D1307608

REWIRE

How To Grow Business
In A Crazy World
And Have A
Great Time Doing It!

JOHN G. ELIASON

You've only been getting part

of the story.

Rewire starts where most other business books end—you've been amazed and entertained, and now you want your piece of the pie. But, have you ever noticed, they never tip their hand quite enough to give you their exact methods to use for your own—

until now.

Rewire is a playbook for winning in business—and enjoying life in the process. You'll learn how to take yourself and your business to the next level, again and again and again…. All in about 100 pages.

- How to get everything you want (page 19)

- Double your business, sales or income—now, with four small adjustments (page 26)

- Simplify (page 31)

- Want more than 2x? Here's the least expensive, highest performing marketing system we've ever used (page 44)

- Build a machine that makes the money (page 51)

- Compress time—day-to-day, minute-by-minute, high-performance "Rewired" schedule (page 67)

- Insurance to get everything you want (page 85)

Finally, methods that work.

WE

are the music makers,
and we
are the dreamers of
DREAMS.

—Willie Wonka

Getting Rewired

Using what you're about to learn, I started from zero—no clients and no money, and in a jam-packed industry. It seems like a crazy thing to do, but there was a method to the madness—there's often tremendous opportunity in a competitive market (look at Apple and iTunes). Today we win awards, generate millions of dollars, and serve thousands of clients nationwide. By the way, we have *no face-to-face meetings* with over ninety percent of our clients or team (by design). Every day, the individuals in my company are deeply committed to the work we do—creating better ways to make the next leap upward as we seek to amaze our clients and multiply them.

What we do is *not* business as usual, at least as most of the world thinks of how traditional business operates. We do what we do *by design*, not because it's what the rest of the world does, but rather because it fits us—this ends up being a very important ingredient in everyone's (yes, everyone's) success. We consciously decided to blend life and business in a way that fuels both. I can't think of a better way to live. This is your challenge to do the same for your life and for your business or career.

Of course every day is a challenge. Challenge is what grows you, and when you rise to it, it's what separates you from the crowd. *Welcome* challenge. Rise to it and live! *Rewire* isn't some sort of fairytale, easy-road, get-rich-quick malarkey. *Rewire* is what you can really do to really get what you want. But enough chatter…

You don't have to just read about it—*you can live it too!*

I'll show you…

What we do is NOT business as usual!

Main Topics

New
to QR
codes?
They are
easy to
use! Download a free QR code scanner app on your smart
phone. Use it to scan the QR code. A website pops up—
watch, read
learn,
and
enjoy.

The Lab is Open

My promise is to deliver to you a guide that you can put to use quickly—a short guide with a big impact. In order to give you precisely the tools you need for success, I have edited out hundreds of pages to make sure that happens. I believe that this guide is better for it.

There's so much more I want to share with you; so much that's cool in the world, so many things just outside the scope of this book, and so many new things that come up on any given day that could be a benefit to your business or life. Our world changes quickly, and you need to run with the most up-to-date tools and techniques. Go to my business-building and lifestyle laboratory, www.rewirelab.org, or scan the QR code below and subscribe (it's free). When you subscribe, you'll get every new update, every new observation and discovery. The lab is the home, the heart, the epicenter of *Rewire* and the evolution of the methods that speed results. This is where you get expanded sessions on specific ideas, experiences, methods—and more resources. Sometimes you really need to hear how something is said or used for greatest effect; at the lab you can see and hear recorded examples of how it's done. And you can watch and listen over and over and over.

www.rewirelab.org

Every time you see the Rewire Lab QR code, it's letting you know that there's more to be found on this subject in the lab.

My books, guides, and the lab are designed to give you fast-track techniques and insight that could take years of trial and error to learn. Now you can read, recognize, install, and course-correct immediately.

Tangled

Life is a great teacher, but it isn't always gentle—far from it. Using the standard business-building sales and marketing techniques the world teaches, I struggled to achieve my dreams. I *thought* I was doing the right thing. I did what I was taught; I studied, practiced, and worked hard, but I found myself struggling—sometimes financially, and sometimes struggling simply to understand the best use of my time. It didn't feel like I was headed in quite the right direction to get the life I really wanted (what I imagined as I drove down the road). It was stressful and disheartening. And I'm not the only one; many people report feeling the same. The methods we've been taught simply are not giving us the results we expect. Something is obviously wrong. Something's mixed up. Something's tangled.

But I wasn't giving up—no way—and I suggest you do the same! I knew that if I could figure this out it would be my ticket to the life I wanted.

I was committed. After all, the quality of my future—my life—depended on it.

So I began. I immersed myself in my journey. I read more books, listened to more speakers, went to seminars, and put myself through more paces than I'd ever allow anyone else to put me through. The books, speakers, courses, and seminars felt promising. They were always entertaining, and some of the techniques even worked. But I found that I still struggled to build in the way I dreamed of. I wanted high profit and low overhead, to be nimble and spirited, and to have a model that allowed me freedom.

It finally dawned on me that I

Many teachers, authors, and speakers have great stories about what they *did*, but very little about what they're *doing*. Of course I like to be entertained as much as the next guy, but I didn't need someone else's glory-day advice, and I didn't need *concept*. I needed someone to say, "Do it like this." Period. Just give me the formula, and I'll go at it day and night to make it work.

Time to Rewire

Finally it dawned on me that either the people talking *really* didn't have the whole recipe, or they weren't sharing some of the critical ingredients I needed to make my world a success. It became evident that those who were experiencing real success were operating methods and systems that were definitely different from what I'd been taught and different from what I was using. I needed to rewire my thinking and my actions!

It wasn't that I was doing poorly, but I needed better, much better, if I were to achieve my dreams. Over time, I'd picked up ideas and methods from some pretty brilliant minds, and I'd re-engineered systems from other industries. My new method came from testing and combining ideas and methods, keeping only what worked really well and discarding what didn't. And all along, I had to continue tweaking. The faster I rewired and tested, the faster the system started coming together. As with any discovery, over time I cracked the code and figured it out. The system didn't all come together overnight; it was years in the making, and it continues to evolve as the world around us evolves, but boy does it work!

This guide is all about transferring that rewired method and system to you—

and then *you* making it even better.

wasn't getting the whole story.

Something You've Never Had

3 Degrees Different

We'll mention the word "different" a lot in this guide. We don't mean bizarre or radically different, but different as in *better*—what we call *3 Degrees Different*. You see this difference all around you. It's the difference between swinging a golf club in a way that sends the ball straight and long, versus a swing that sends a ball into the next fairway. Those subtle differences, over time, can lead to either the Poor Farm or Millionaire Acres. Just a three-degree shift can spell the difference between living a life of "I'm glad I did" rather than "I wish I had." The differences are subtle, very intentional, and can make a huge impact on your quality of life. 3 Degrees Different is a cornerstone of *Rewire*.

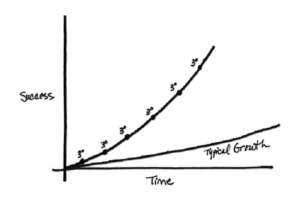

3 Degrees Different is why this book is *intentionally short*. What you see here is about one-third the size of the original—and much better because of it. Because there is so much competition for your attention, we need to be brief and brilliant: You need to be able to put these methods into action fast. The methods you find here are real; they work. I know because we use them every day—it's exactly how we launched, built, and went from zero to hero in our businesses and lives. This is also how we continue to grow an amazing business in a constantly evolving and crazy world.

What You've Done So Far is Perfect

You have been operating perfectly to achieve exactly what you have right now. You do what you do perfectly—congratulations! And you will continue to have exactly what you have now, give or take, as long as you continue to use the same beliefs, thoughts, methods, techniques, rituals, and habits. Interestingly, that understanding actually gives some of us a little comfort. It's like, "Hey, I may not be getting what I want, but at least I'm comfortable doing it." Others often report an "Ah-ha!" moment, understanding clearly that they must do things a bit differently if they want something more in business or life. If you choose to operate differently, it will feel different at first. All things do—even clasping your hands with left thumb over right—versus right over left—feels awkward if you're used to doing it the other way. (Try it!) So, even small tweaks feel awkward at first. But massive change can come from small adjustments—just 3 Degrees Different.

A Better Tomorrow, Today

Do I have *all* the answers for you? Not by a long shot. What I do have, and what I will be giving you here, are the methods that we've found to work, period. What you learn here is how we operate and how we generate very high profit from very low overhead,. And it's ready for you to apply to your situation. For over two decades, my team and I have been asking hard questions and pilot-testing better ways that lead to success. I've had the great pleasure of seeing many people use these methods to achieve more than they thought possible—and by "more," I mean more of *everything*, including money, satisfaction, feelings of accomplishment, and a rewarding quality of life. That's why I am positive that the insights and methods in this guide will be valuable to you as

"If you *want* something you've never had, you must be willing to *do* something you've never done."

—Thomas Jefferson

you launch or grow your business and create the best and most meaningful life for yourself and those you care about.

Furthermore, I won't claim that my ways are *the only ways*. There are really a lot of super cool businesses opportunities and methods out there—amazing ideas and processes that actually work! The problem is that there's also a sea of outdated and short-sighted ways of going about business that just won't get you very far. And, I have to be honest, most of what I see falls into the latter category. The trick is to sort out what's a good opportunity, plan, or method, and what's not—what works and what doesn't. But without experience or a lot of time and extreme drive, it's not that easy to distinguish between the two. Sorting through it all can easily take decades. Figuring it all out—finding what works—may never happen for you. That would be a shame.

My job here is to take both what my team and I have learned and what I see every day in business and transfer it to you, so you can shorten your success learning curve to a fraction of what it would be if you set out alone. My job is to help you understand the best methods, so you can start enjoying your better tomorrow, today.

As you begin reading this guide, you may find yourself wondering,"Do I have to quit my current job to get what I want? Do I have to change careers? Start my own business? Or, if I own my own business, do I need to completely revamp my business plan?" The answer to all those questions is, "*Read on*, before you even think about making those kinds of decisions." What I'm going to show you in this guide will help you get from *where you are now* to *where you want to go*, no matter what business you're in, no matter whether you're the low man or woman on the totem pole, building a clientele, managing a team, or the CEO.

Whatever stage you are at in life or business, you can learn these strategies quickly and launch these methods immediately to absolutely shorten the time it takes you to get where you want to go.

So…where's a good place to start?

Let's take a look at some of the observable *different* behaviors between successfully rewired folks and everyone else.

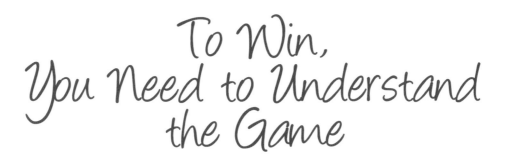

Succeeding in business, or life for that matter, without understanding the game is about as likely as winning the lottery. Sure, a few do win, but as a plan, it's not a good one. Understand and apply the basics of your game to assure your winning.

The Crowd vs. the Rewired

Like most concepts that have stood the test of time, the 80:20 Rule sounds simple, but it's real and it's important. The danger is that we've heard it so many times that it's easy to gloss over it. Do yourself a life favor and consider this concept for a moment. It's foundational. Understand how it operates within human nature and how you can give yourself an instant advantage at the 80:20 crossroads.

You've heard it before, but go slow here. First, a definition: The 80:20 Rule says that 80 percent of all the good stuff—everything from money and happiness to the best schools for your kids and the coolest travel destinations on Earth—goes to only 20 percent of the population. The top 20 percent get nearly all of it; the rest divide up what's left.

What do I call people who are in the 80 percent? The Crowd.

And the top 20 percent? The Rewired.

$400,000 vs. $25,000

You may be saying, "Hey, no big deal—I'm okay being part of the Crowd. I'm still going to make 20 percent of what the movers and shakers earn." But hold on—that's not how the math works, nor how it works in real life.

Let's look at a real scenario where we have $1,000,000 that is going to be divided up among ten people. It may surprise you to realize that if you're one of the Crowd, your payday is $25,000. If you're Rewired, your payday is $400,000— that's 16 times more!

Payday Calculator

$1,000,000 to be paid out:

20% to the Crowd = $200,000
8 people in the Crowd divide up $200,000 and get $25,000 each

80% to the Rewired = $800,000
2 Rewireds divide $800,000 and get $400,000 each.

Which payday do you want?

That's right, *16 times more money* goes to the people who have rewired their thinking. They are the committed, purpose-filled people who simply and consciously use the methods that work better than average. And that's not just math, that's how we see real life work.

What Does it Mean to be in the Crowd?

 If you're in the Crowd, you go with the flow. You do what's "normal." You do what 80 percent of the population does. You don't ask many questions, but you complain that things aren't as you'd like. It's easy to be a member of the Crowd. Just do what everyone around you is doing, think like they're thinking, say what they're saying, and *voilà* you're there. In the Crowd you get pretty much what everyone else gets—a prepackaged, one-size-fits-all life.

Life Rewired

Living Rewired is all about choosing your own path, designing your own life and then deciding how to fund it. You can be Rewired inside someone else's company or by having your own. The critical piece is making it *your* choice. Living Rewired comes with plenty of challenges, and overcoming them is your price of admission into a world that the majority of all the population only gets to glimpse.

If you want all the gold and all the freedom, you'll challenge yourself, ask yourself different questions, and operate 3 Degrees Differently. Those three degrees, over distance, can mean the difference between an awesome lifestyle and a mediocre existence. Living Rewired, you'll actually find yourself intentionally looking *away* from the crowd. The methods in this guide are the ways people operate who want the money, lifestyle, freedom—all the good stuff.

So if some of the techniques you're about to learn seem just a little foreign to you, and you've never made a high income over a long period of time— or enjoyed life in the process—you may want to take that as a hint that you may need to consider operating differently. I strongly suggest you test these techniques, try them on, and find out how they work.

It's all about choosing your own...

Build the Machine, and Then Let it Do the Work

 The Crowd works without a whole lot of leverage or multiplication of effectiveness. Rewireds operate 3 Degrees Differently. Rewireds will tell you, "I'll work day and night to build a machine (think machine, method, system) that helps me multiply my reward or make my work easier." Rewireds know they need to build and tweak the system before it will work for them. It's like having to build the airplane before you get the benefit of flight. But once you've built the plane and you can fly—wow, does that change life! And that's exactly what this system has done for me, our company, and many others. I know that if you put in the energy and intention required, using these methods and this system will most certainly change the quality of your life.

Scan this code to go to the lab and learn about the type of machines we love to create!

Will You Choose to be Free?

That old saying, "You reap what you sow" is true! You get out of it what you put in. When you are committed, passionate, and operating with a purpose, it's reflected in your income, your lifestyle, and the quality of life you can provide for the people you love. Interestingly, few actually operate in a mindful balance this way. Certainly, most of your competition does not. So when you do—congratulations! You're operating 3 Degrees from normal, and you're on the right track.

You can be whoever and whatever you want in life. It's easy to be nonchalant, but it's also easy to be engaged, determined, committed, and excited! Sometimes we just don't understand what it takes to live Rewired, but read on, because the methods in this guide show you *exactly* how many do it.

What do you want...

And something else: Be at the top of the Rewired heap, and you also get *freedom*. Freedom to pretty much do whatever you like. If you want to be free, then this guide is for you!

How To Get Everything That You Want

It's amazing to see the difference in lifestyles people can create for themselves when they actually have their mind working *for* them. Wow. It's a critical foundational element of the game. All the techniques and tricks in the world aren't going to do you much long-term good unless your mind is on your side. But how? The problem is that we're simply not taught to think in a way that gets us what we want—it's one of the biggest reasons we fail to become Rewired and get stuck in the Crowd. We want more, but our brains and conditioning get in our way. The good news is that there are a few mental tools you can use to rewire immediately. We'll start right off the bat with some of the biggest leverage you can get.

What do you want…really? It's a short question, but it has big impact.

 Most of us never get what we want because we don't really *know* what we want. Most of us do what's expected; we go to college, we get "good jobs," and we live life based on what our job provides. We do the best we can for ourselves and our families with what we earn. But sooner or later, at some point we start to wish we'd done it differently. We wish we had more money, time, and freedom. We wish we could spend more time with people we love. And we wish we were doing something that we truly enjoy. We wish we had made different

...really?

choices and designed our lives just a bit better. Ask anyone over forty, and they'll tell you this is one hundred percent true. The great news is, it's not too late. You can start designing and living better today.

Do an Einstein

We've found that people who have massive success do what Albert Einstein did: they question everything. Though these successful people are scheduled, intentional, and diligent, they are also questioning and full of wonder—they're curious, and  they test those curiosities. The person who asks high-quality questions—not just sometimes but *all* the time—ends up heading in a slightly different direction than most folks. Continuing to ask those high-quality questions and tweaking direction just 3 Degrees with each answer, compounds the change in direction. Folks that "do an Einstein" soon find themselves in a whole different world.

People who don't ask questions stay on the same no-growth curve, and they wonder why they lack the success and life they really want.

In our world today, those who find success in business, sports, and science—those who "do an Einstein"—have an almost philosophical approach to their craft. They don't necessarily take what the rest of the world believes is "fact" as fact. After all, maybe 1 stick + 1 stick doesn't really equal 2 sticks. (What if you took one of those sticks and broke it in half? New result! Three sticks!) Maybe their predecessors didn't ask effective enough questions or have the right tools to find the best answers to be used as their truths. They ask themselves how 1+1 could = 3, 4, 5, or 17? They ask themselves:

"How can I think or operate just a bit differently and come to a completely different answer?"

Then they test the tool. The new result becomes their upgraded operating, sales, marketing, and customer service process.

Most of us are never going to have the same impact on the world as Einstein. But the impact we can have on our own businesses and lives can be huge. I asked myself a high-quality question a few years ago. It was, "How can I double my income and have a good time doing it?" I kept asking this question. Within two years my business more than doubled, and so did my income! My next question was, "How can I continue to make this level of income with only half the effort?" I figured out that answer, too!

Two times the money and one half the effort? I liked that equation!

I decided Einstein was on to something, and I started asking myself all kinds of questions! You can do the same.

Hear, but Don't Listen

Here's another one…and we can put it to use immediately. Be aware of your own self-talk—you know, those voices you hear in your head that probably are not helping you achieve your dream. Like that voice saying: "I've heard all this stuff before. Sure it might work, but do I really want to go through all the effort?" Or the voice that says, "Being in the Crowd is okay! After all, my parents and grandparents were part of the Crowd and they were good people, so there's nothing wrong with being there." Or maybe you have a little voice saying, "Hey, I only have sixteen years left before I retire, so I think I'll just hang in there with my 'good job.'"

Hear those voices? People in the Crowd let their weird self-talk run unchecked; it rules their behavior and their life. It's damn dangerous. Rewireds, on the other hand, have a different mindset. Rewireds will say:

Be aware of your own self-talk…

"Hey, you're right, I do have all kinds of goofy things running through my mind. Maybe I can test seeding my brain with stuff that actually empowers me, and see how that works."

You may find yourself starting to be aware of the negativity that flows through your mind and swap it for positive stuff that helps you achieve your dream.

You may even start asking yourself *3 Degrees Different* questions like: "How can I double my income, have more freedom, and have a great time doing it?" The answers you get back from your brain are interesting.

Go ahead. Try it on right now. See what your brain comes back with. Most people report they get a positive feeling, like more things in life are possible...and they also get a few new ideas. That's what it means to start thinking like a Rewired. So do it: Grab a pad of paper, ask yourself the question again, and begin writing. See how ideas start popping?

Using your Dream, as Leverage, Against Yourself

What?! Now that just *sounds* weird. But remember, we're human, and we *are* a bit weird. You need to use a combination of the carrot and the stick on yourself. Use a bit of pain and a bit of pleasure and...*voilà*! Here's how it works.

Do this exercise:

First, you've got to imagine how it feels getting what you want. Imagine all those goals. Picture it; feel what it will feel like to have it. Imagine how you (and your kids, if you have them) look on the beach—all tan and laughing. Imagine yourself in good physical shape. Imagine how you'll feel driving that car. Imagine how it feels to know you make more money than anyone else in the room, how it feels to have no money worries, to be able to travel as much as you want and give to those in need, whatever it is for you. You get the idea. Think it, see it, and feel it. Really *feeling* it is critical here. So really get into it, anchor those feelings of happiness, accomplishment, and pride deep in your chest. Really let yourself feel it. The deeper you feel it, the faster you'll get what you want.

Don't stop there! Keep imagining how bright and clean and happy your life will be as you enjoy your days living your lifestyle design, having achieved your goals. It feels great, right? If it doesn't feel great, then you've set your goals too low, and they're simply not exciting enough for you to really want to achieve. You need to have a spectacular dream, one that makes you feel like there's nothing that will stop you from living it—like it's the coolest life you could possibly have. It makes you feel giddy to imagine it could be yours—and you will do anything to achieve it.

So, raise the excitement bar. And once you are crazy excited to achieve your newly designed lifestyle…stop! Switch gears.

Now imagine how dismal an experience life would be if you never achieved your goals. What a disappointment life would be to you (and to the others around you) to have wanted those goals so badly and to have never achieved them. The kids didn't get to the beach. You stayed fat even when you could have been slim, you never got the car, you never traveled, you never were able to help those in need, you never got the experience…all those things in life you dreamed of just never came true for you.

If imagining that doesn't make you want to cry or puke, your dream isn't important enough to you—go back and set the bar higher, choose more heartfelt, meaningful goals. You must have goals that you feel, that are emotionally *charged*—not just the kind of goals that you know intellectually. You must *feel* them. You must want them so badly that not achieving makes you feel absolutely horrible despair, disgust, deep sadness, and grief. You must experience *feeling* the highs of having and the lows of not having. Emotion is what drives you. Use it.

So, design your life. Get connected with the feeling of achieving it—that's your carrot. But also get connected with the feeling of never having achieved it and feel what a dark, bile-filled life that would be—that's your stick. When you feel yourself getting casual or sluggish, use one or both of these on yourself—whichever one incites you to more action at the time. It works if you want it to work. However, if you're just going to go about this life design thing casually, don't do any of this stuff, put down this book, and you'll get what everyone else gets. But if you want it all, *you have to get leverage on yourself.*

Now when things don't go as planned, you have the drive, the reasons, the "whys" linked emotionally, and you're more likely to get back on the horse. The lack of deeply linked emotional "whys" is the reason most people quit (diets included).

The Fear Factor

If the formula is so clear, then why don't we all have what we want? Answer: fear. Fear of *doing* it. Fear of *not* doing it. Fear of *what-if-it-doesn't-work*. And fear of *what-happens-when-it-does-work*. We humans are chock full of fears. That's just how it is. The cool thing is, once we know it's there and that we all have it, we can recognize it for what it is. Once you shine a light on it and recognize it and label it, you'll feel better because it's now tangible and you're able to manage it and move past it.

Again, the intent of this guide isn't to dive into this area any further than pointing out that you're human and it's okay. The trick is how to understand your fear—even use your fear to your advantage.

Using Fear To Get What You Want

When you're afraid, it's usually about something you're unsure of, right? But then when you finally move forward and realize *it wasn't really that scary after all,* you no longer have fear. Your action dissolved your fear.

So, now, when you hear that little voice in your head say things like, "This isn't for you," or "Just do it later," you know that it's simply fear talking to you. And now you know the trick to turn fear into a friend: Whenever you hear those little voices, be aware, notice the fear, acknowledge it. Notice fear talking and then tell yourself, "Ah-ha, I hear fear talking, that's my cue to move/act/ do." Let the fear be a trigger to perform an action that takes you closer to your goal.

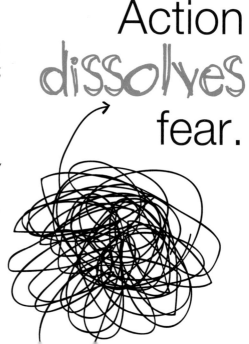

Action dissolves fear.

And there you have it—you just figured out how to use fear to get what you want. Bring on the fear!

Plans Don't Go as Planned—They Go Better!

If you're excited about the proposition of a new venture and designing a cool lifestyle and looking for a guaranteed smooth ride, here's a bucket of cold candor on your scheme. It's just one of the funny little tricks life plays on all of us—our plans don't quite go as planned, but that's OK.

And what about *your plan*, the one that you hope to achieve in five years? It will never happen. At least it won't happen the way you spent countless hours planning it would. Sometimes it happens more quickly. Often it takes bit longer than anticipated. Why? Because life and learning happen the way they *need* to. There may be lessons along the way that will make you better, stronger, and faster in more ways than one, lessons that will serve you as you grow and prosper. Strange, but true.

So we need to make course corrections as we go. Often those corrections require a little time. That's not a bad thing—it's actually *necessary* because we're learning something valuable that we need to understand before we can go forward. Then, when we do go forward, we have the knowledge and ability required to get to the end. (Sounds like a movie plot, doesn't it?) So the timeframe sometimes gets a bit longer, but the monstrous unexpected benefit of adjusting as you go is that you actually achieve your goals—and you end up with a cooler life than your plan originally called for!

It's Time to Make Your Dream Real!

This guide can help you break free and control your time effectively, and enjoy your life; not every second of every day, but a lot more than you're probably experiencing today. And, at the same time, you'll make more money and live a more vibrant life than most. You'll know how to get clear about your goals, how to achieve them, and how to enjoy the journey.

So, you want to make real money and live a very cool lifestyle? Yes? If so, then welcome to the first day of the rest of your life, my friend. Let's begin.

Dump the Struggle, Double Your Money

Traditional Marketing: Uncertain Return on Investment

Most marketing campaigns, especially if new, almost never give an immediate positive return on investment. In other words, most new marketing campaigns lose money. That's tough, especially for those of us in new ventures and high expectations.

The same is true with new businesses—most go bust, as do most entrepreneurs, marketers, and sales people—the numbers are staggering. Working with 20,000 business operators, sales people, and entrepreneurs for a quarter century, it's easy to see why—we're taught wrong. We're given the wrong expectations, improper understanding and expectations, ineffective techniques and outdated direction.

We're not "taught wrong" on purpose, of course: it seems to be more a function of a downward spiral of training over time.

A lot of training, especially sales, seems designed not to educate you so you understand what you're doing, but rather to give you the minimal information necessary to lever out a few sales as quickly as possible, burn you out, and then hire a new wave of sales people. Other longer, more formal training is simply worn out and doesn't work well enough today. And often it's the trainers who are the ones who *sound* like they know what they're talking about, but who have never really had success themselves.

The end result? For decades, you and I have been getting diluted training that has devolved into practices that just are not very effective.

 The truth is, there are simply a few more pieces to the real success formula than what's being taught. There's additional information you need to have the pieces snap into place.

Everyone wants success, but the big questions for everyone who wants to grow are, "*Where* do I start?," "*Whom* do I target?," "*Where* do I go?," and "*What* do I do?" We see most everyone starts in a sort of blunt instrument, expensive, slow, outdated, low-return, low-leverage with uncertain end results, sales and marketing efforts. They grasp at straws with a series of dead-end methods often based on what they were taught at a previous job or how they see the Crowd operate. Here's what we see everyone (98%) do:

1. **Warm marketing**, which is great, except that everyone usually gets to the end of their city or warm market, and that's where their business comes to a grinding halt—and they're done.

2. **Cold calling**, even with thick skin, gets old fast. Typical cold call numbers go like this: Of 100 contacts, 90 say, "No." In fact they may say this very aggressively. 10 will be

"Those who can't *do*, teach. And those who can't teach, teach gym."

—Jack Black, *School of Rock*

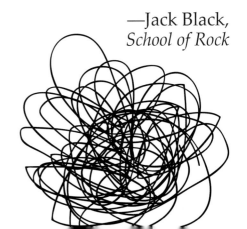

interested, and 2 will become clients, and then you start all over again next week. It's a lot of abuse for little reward. The prospect of doing this forever drives most people to quit.

3. **Advertising** (print, direct mail, online) is usually very expensive and often doesn't pay enough return on the first or second or third run, and there's no more money to continue testing. If you have enough money and time to figure it out, you'll need to continue to experiment for good return, forever.

4. **Networking groups**, Chamber of Commerce, etc. At this level we've advanced a bit and are thinking about warmer leads. That's a good thing. It's better than cold calling, and that's a relief, so we often stop here thankful that we found a happier place. But wait, don't get too complacent! Where's the real growth, bigger business, and designed lifestyle that we're really looking for?

For years, I and my businesses operated exactly that way. We did what everyone else does—had nifty (so we thought) graphics created, bought lists, mailed, advertised, cold called, networked, hired supposed consultants, bought marketing systems. We did all the things that you're taught to do. Some things actually worked okay. But each of these methods had a low return on investment: the time, money, and energy investment just don't produce what you want. And they all have short hang times—the amount of time your marketing stays "in the air," active and producing business before it runs out of gas and hits the ground. The shorter the hang time, the less valuable your marketing; the longer the hang time, the more valuable. The high response and long hang time we wanted—and the success levels we craved—always seemed to be just out of reach. We wanted long hang time, but usually it felt like our airplane had only one wing. We needed something better, and we found it!

Rewired Marketing: Clear Targets, High Success, High Profit

With years of questioning (doing Einsteins)—testing, tweaking, and striving—we finally figured it out: the reason all these standard ways weren't working so well was because we were given only half the recipe. If you want to make the old ways work, you need the whole picture—you need the missing ingredients. You need the other wing. With this following knowledge in action we accelerated our growth and *income*, and so can you. Here's what we found:

1. **Warm marketing:** Thinking of these folks as "tier one" works fantastically when you understand the real value of your warm market:

   a. You get a couple fast sales now, and then a few more down the road. We call these initial targets that could be buyers, *Prospects*.

   b. But the huge value is really your warm market's warm market! It's tier two, three, and four. We found that having a plan to catapult beyond our first tier of warm contacts and into their warm markets multiplied the value of our warm market. This trick has made for some of our most profitable business—ever. Adding a system for tracking these connections increased warm market value and locked it in as our preferred method of doing business. We call those who refer us to their contacts *Referrers*.

2. **Cold Calling:** The problem with traditional cold calling is that it's about 60 percent less effective today than just a few years ago. It's not that we're different, but the environment sure is, and we need to adapt. Today, more than ever before, with door-to-door and tele-sales armies from everyone around the globe, our prospects don't know who to trust, so they trust nobody—including you and me. Another factor you must weigh is the deluge of hundreds of TV channels, internet news, newspapers, magazine, newsletter, email, texting, and social media bombardment we all experience. Our brains don't like all this noise, and we start filtering out a lot of it. Some of those filters will screen out you and me. If you're in a competitive industry and are cold calling, you're up against some interesting new challenges. To succeed you need to operate 3 Degrees Different from the crowd, otherwise you're treated just like everyone else—that's not good for your business. Because it takes time to establish trust, the old one-

It takes time to establish trust...

cold-call close may now be a three- or five-call close. If the process takes longer, how do you afford the time it takes to keep connecting, to build trust, when there's just not that much money to be made on one sale?

   a. Poor sales, great marketing: The answer we found is that cold calling just isn't good sales technique anymore, but it can be great marketing! When we finally figured out that 90-95% percent of all calls are really marketing or seed-planting calls, the pressure was off and the calls became more part of an intentional systematized series of calls that built trust. You need to recalibrate your expectations and sales projections if you choose to operate this way, because sales just take longer.

   b. Voicemail: We found that we leave a lot more messages today compared to just a few years ago. The way you leave a message needs to be well thought out, practiced, and executed. You may want to do an Einstein here and ask yourself, "What kind of message do I need to leave to get them to call me back before they return any other calls and have them leaning forward wanting to hear what I have to say?" Be careful to not leave a too-sensational message here: if you do, you burn their trust in you.

3. **Advertising** (print, direct mail, online) often doesn't pay off quickly or directly—or ever at all. But if we bought advertising and then added direct marketing (including cold calls and email) related to that advertising, then we can increase response rates and maybe even make it pay off. (Example: What if we *first advertise* in a banking magazine and then call bankers and say, "Yeah, you probably saw us this month in *ABC Bankers Magazine*....")

   a. Now the banker feels we're more credible because he actually saw us in the magazine. We had to point it out, but that's better than hoping he saw us.

   b. It was probably cheaper to advertise in the magazine and call than to send a mailer to every banker.

   c. We can send emails with a picture of the ad from the magazine—also cheap.

   d. If we wanted to cold call market to bankers, this would warm the call up quickly. The call is more of a, "Hey, I'm following up on our piece on page

59 of *ABC Bankers Magazine*…." It's a great ice breaker and turns the call to cool rather than cold—much better!

    e.   We don't have to advertise every month in the overly expensive bankers magazine to have the credibility we just gained with one month's advertising and good solid follow-up.

4. **Networking groups**, Chamber of Commerce, etc. Here too, the only way to make your contacts better is to work them smarter—which means more aggressively, and with a system.

    a.   When you're involved in the Chamber of Commerce and other membership groups where members are prospects, you have interests in common with other members of the group. Almost everyone expects to be targeted as a Prospect or a Referrer by other members of the group, and that's okay. So do it! Your contacts in these groups are easier sales because you're in the same club, but don't take that to mean that you can cut corners on good sales technique—you can't. Do a great job and you'll get business here. Multiply your results with systematic follow-up: this is *key* to compounding growth that we'll explain in detail soon.

    b.   In networking groups you basically trade contacts, so what you get is a very light referral. These contacts are much better than a cold contact. It's easy to call up these folks and say, "Hey, my friend Shelley suggested I may be able to help you [enter the benefit of what you sell]."

Revolving Systems Make Business Easier and Life Better

There's one more basic yet critical element you must have to leave the crowd behind—*order*. By that we mean an effective system for following up, cultivating, nurturing your prospects. It's critical. The best systems for follow-up are revolving—day-to-day, month-to-month, and year-to-year. They never end. They never stop working for you.

Recently I was talking with a woman—an entrepreneur with a focus in sales, who said, "I have the best job in the world; I love it! But I need to make more money. I need to use my time better. I just can't quite seem to get on track with what I'm supposed to do every day. I think if I could get that on track I'd do a lot better." Having a little insight into whom she contacts and how she does business, I asked about a list of prospects I knew she'd started working a while back. She said, "Yeah, I went through that list and got a few accounts." That was over a year ago. I asked if she'd gone back through that list again. The answer was, "No, but I've been meaning to." Ah *ha*!

Use your brain for those things that pay the most, like communication. Let systems do the work that pays less, like organization.

Systems don't need to be complicated. You can make your fortune using a simple system. We see so many people miss their fortune by getting mired in impressive-sounding systems that end up going unused

Systems dont need to be

because they have long learning curves. Elaborate systems often have too many elements that just get in the way of making money and take too long to set up. The most absolutely effective starter system we've ever used is a combination of a calendar, a revolving "tickler file" system, and ranking every contact in rotation. It's absolutely old-school (don't worry, we'll show you high-tech too), but we used this system for years, and it's a great place to start, even with all the technology available today. It looks like this:

 Calendar—We like those 12-month journal-looking books with an entire week at a glance across two pages. Here's how we found it best to use this kind of calendar:

- The *only* notes that go in the calendar are for appointments, period.

- You look at your calendar at the beginning of each day and then periodically throughout the day to see when you have scheduled calls or appointments.

- Have only one calendar. (More than one is too confusing.)

- The only good notes in a calendar are observations about life and experience. Keep all your calendars forever so you can look back at your life: it's really a cool journey.

- Keep contact information, history, and other information *out* of your calendar. (Use a revolving tickler file for everything except appointments.)

Tickler File—You have a total of 43 hanging files. Thirty-one of those files have tabs on the top labeled with the numbers "1" through "31": that's one file for each day of the month. Add 12 more hanging files—one for each month of the year—and you're set. Here's how it works:

complicated.

• Each one of your contacts, targets, or prospects has a note card, recipe card, piece of paper, bar napkin, or something with their information written on it. That information includes the person's name, phone number, email address (we'll discuss the use of email later), notes about the person's life (i.e. "son loves lacrosse" or "daughter goes to Iowa State"), and history of your contact with the person (what you discussed on the call and where you're trying to take this prospect).

- If today is October 12, I open up the file that says "12." In there are all kinds of these contact sheets for people whom I previously decided that I needed to call today, the 12th. Now I know exactly who I need to contact today. Before the start of the day (or the night before), I sifted through everything and arranged my contacts in order of how I want to deal with them. (I may also have stuck a list in here from months ago, reminding myself that it's time to go back through that list again.) As I go through my stack of contacts, I'm having conversations and making notes and refiling the contact sheet for later. If I make a call and the prospect's not in, I can put the sheet a little deeper in my stack for a repeat call. That repeat call could occur in an hour or so when I get to it, or at the end of day, or tomorrow (if I put it in the file labeled 13), or next week (in one of the files labeled 18-25). If I'm going to call again next month, the sheet goes into one of the files numbered 1-11 (to be opened in days 1-11 of the next month).

Or, if I'm thinking about what I will do 4 to 8 weeks from now, I put the sheet into a folder for next month (in this case, November).

- Tomorrow, I open up file 13 and do the same. And so on for days 14, 15, and 16. At the beginning of the month I open up the new month's folder, scan through my contacts, look at my notes and history, and file them in the number files accordingly (for example, "Call Jim on November 27" goes in 27). Pretty simple stuff, and you can use it right away.

Ranking—The Rewired rank everyone. An easy system is A-B-C. Think of this ranking as the likelihood that you're going to do business with someone or get a referral from them. The As (top 10 percent) are likely,

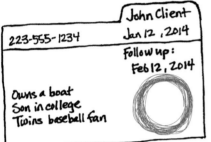

so you want to make sure you keep in better contact with them than Bs or Cs. When you open your file for the day, it's easy to sort out who to call first—As, then Bs, and finally Cs.

And there it is, a simple, silly, little system that can make you a fortune. Why does it work? It works because it simply keeps you on track. It keeps you consistently contacting the people you need to in an orderly fashion. Oh, and that entrepreneur from the story above, the one who wasn't following up the way she knew she should? Since she was introduced to this simple little system, she's gotten back on track and become confident again.

Consistent Action Creates Fortunes

The Rewired operate consistently—we see it all the time. The Crowd doesn't. It's hard to get traction and success when you dabble. You don't need to work 90 hours a week, but you do need to plan some consistency. You've heard of people making a quiet, part-time fortune or launching their business on their lunch hour. It can really be done! Even a little time daily works better than, "I'll go at it hard over the holidays or on my week off next month." Your success plan needs to include ongoing, consistent action.

ReMarketing™

Have you ever switched from one company to another for something you buy? For example, have you ever switched mobile phone service from one company to another? Most people answer, "Yes." Did you plan to switch when you started a new service? The answer is almost always, "No." The point is that people change. They change their ideas, they switch services and buy products that they never expected to or said "no" to at one point. Here's the question: "When they're ready to switch, change, and buy, do you want to be there so they can buy from you, or would you rather someone else get the business?"

Hey, out of sight out of mind! Stay on their mind by staying in touch—creatively. Be there so you can get the business.

We've found that you should connect with each of your contacts every 14 to 45 days. We call this ReMarketing™. If you're operating the file system described above, you pull out everyone and call them. You can probably keep up with about 20 percent of all your contacts. Reach out with a live call only the ones who are most likely to do business with you. Those are the As, *then* the Bs, and finally the Cs (Cs only if you have time). Then follow up with an email so they have your contact info when they need you, or so they have it close at hand to be able to give to someone else who can use you. That's why you always want their email address. If you're using software to house and arrange your calendar and contacts, then all you need to do is tell it to create lists, and plan your calls from the lists that are generated. (We'll cover this in detail later.)

Creative Contact

 When you get Creative, you get remembered, and people like you. Our research has found that the best sales and ReMarketing™ results come from connections that are brief, creative, and customized to the prospect's interest—that means no generic, tired, old-fashioned newsletters. (We'll cover the reasons why later.) The big thing is to act; just do it.

Here are some Creative Contact ReMarketing™ ideas for various businesses—they can be phone, mail, or email:

- **Retail**—We understand that location is "everything," but that's also retail's big downfall: you grab a great location and then wait. Waiting seems like a dangerous business plan. How about amping up and leveraging some direct marketing techniques to assure your win? Some do, and they do it very well. The best example is my favorite men's clothing store in Plymouth, Minnesota. They call me every 60-90 days. I always let their call go to voicemail, but it prompts me to swing by when I'm in the neighborhood. In fact, just now, as I was writing, they called to let me know the three pairs of pants I bought after their last call have been tailored and are ready for pickup. I've spent thousands of dollars there that I certainly wouldn't have without their call. I have a nicer wardrobe, and I can refer others—which I do when people ask where I bought the shark shorts, or the wild winter coat, or the awesome blue suit. I'm glad they call.

- **Mortgage**— "Hey John, just touching base. You've seen rates are low, but does it make dollars and sense to you right now? Ask yourself these 3 questions to know for sure, then call me if you'd like to explore a bit more."

- **Credit card processing**—You can have an app that allows you to take credit cards from your mobile device. This is a great way to increase your business while making transactions convenient for your customers.

- **Dentist**— "We know sometimes there's a bit of a wait to see Dr. Molar; how about getting whiter teeth in the process? Ask about our new 30-minute teeth-whitening system. Call us to add it to your next visit."

- **Real estate**— "Hey, want to take a peek at your neighbor's house? They just listed it for sale and tomorrow there's an open house."

- **Cars**— "You're probably not in the market, but we just took a black 911 4S in on trade—it's a blast! You've got to come test drive it!"

- **Veterinarian**— "New pet spa! Drop off your furry family member for a free afternoon."

The point of all these creative messages is to make sure your clients and prospects think of *you* first when they're ready to buy. Simple, short, creative, and consistent is often the best advertising.

 See more ideas for Creative Contact in the Lab!

It Works! What a Relief!

With the full recipe, a calendar, a system for follow-up, ranking, creative contact, and ReMarketing™ all running, it's easy to imagine simply having a lot more success than most, and we do. So does everyone we've ever met who follows this system. Honestly, it's a relief to finally have methods that work! Finally, a clear plan that steers directly toward success. No more *wondering* if it was going to work. It works!

That's it. That's really all we (and most everyone) needs to do to lock in success and double their results and income. These simple differences are what almost always separate the successes from those who quit, fail, or bail. Just add the missing ingredients and *voilà*, it works! Like most answers usually are when you finally figure them out, they're simple and they make complete sense.

Make these methods your own and you've just taken one giant step to significantly increasing your income, value, independence, and freedom.

No more wondering—it works!

The
SYSTEM
is
the

solution.

—IBM

The System Is The Solution

Not Sexy, but It Is Effective!

I know, it's out of fashion, but if you want real success, then you need a system that actually works. In our click-and-make-a-million, infomercial world, the old hanging file system may not look sexy—but it works, it's easy, and it will make you money. Learn the system from an old-school level, and it will make a lot more sense—you'll be so much more empowered when you hyper-speed this system with awesome software. And yes, very soon we'll show you how to take this system to the stratosphere with the right software. We live in that stratosphere, and we'll show you exactly how to get there too.

 Another fantastic benefit of understanding the system before going high-tech is that you're never at the mercy of anyone's software limits, the latest online marketing craze, or the next here-today-gone-tomorrow social media frenzy.

When you understand the system, you own that knowledge and can apply it—no matter what the technology of the day is—to any business, any time, and any place. You can use to it create real wealth.

As soon as you get the basics nailed down, your system will begin working for you immediately. That's what you want.

Fast Launch, Low Overhead, High Profit

Our illustration starts at ground zero—how to launch the system, who to contact first, and the proper timing. You'll launch in Warm Marketing (always an excellent place to start). All additional marketing methods fall into the same system; this will make even more sense as you continue through the guide.

It's time to start. We've already described the hanging file system with the 43 hanging files. Now, be sure to get something to hold the files. You can buy a wire rack built for holding hanging files when you pick up your file folders, or you can use all kinds of other options—a milk crate, a file cabinet, a box, or whatever. But that's not important now. (You can order it later, pick it up tomorrow.) Right now, it's important to grab a stack of paper, a pad, note/index/recipe cards, bar napkins—anything, really. Right now is the time to get your contacts down on paper. First things first!

Zero In

Remember in Warm Marketing how we had *Prospects* and *Referrers*. Now's the time to get them out of your head, onto paper, and into your system.

Start with contacts you're familiar with—that's friends, family, and people-at-businesses. Pull together all your lists, including holiday cards, phone, email, Facebook. Think of everyone you do business with, places you shop…everyone! Most people find they have at least 150 to 200 contacts. If you sell a business product or service, maybe 15 percent could be Prospects—potential clients. The other 85 percent will be potential Referrers. If you sell a product or service that everyone can buy, you simply have a lot more Prospects up front.

Grab those cards or sheets of paper, one for each contact. You're going to make three piles of contacts: A Prospects, B Prospects, and Referrers:

1. **A Prospects:** You have a relationship with these people. They can be friends, family, or very close acquaintances, and they buy what you sell or probably would buy what you sell.

Example: If I were selling mortgages, nearly all my friends, family, and acquaintances would be A Prospects, since most are home owners and probably have mortgages that I could refinance (or they could use me when they buy a new property). If I were selling business phone systems, only those in business or those who were looking at going into business would be A Prospects. These first Prospects will *also* become your first Referrers—two birds, one stone.

Because you make money by selling, not by making piles of contact cards, it's time to contact your A Prospects. Stop writing out cards and making piles—start making contact. When you do, one of two things is going to happen: your Prospect will buy, or they won't. When they buy, you now have a Client *and* a Referrer. Be sure to ask for Referrals and put everyone back into your system for follow-up. If they don't buy, don't fret. Maybe the timing wasn't right. (How many times have you said, "No," only to later say, "Yes"?) Still, ask for referrals, then put them back in your system as a Prospect and a Referrer. Contact their referrals right away and make sure everyone is in your system. Place them in the proper folder for the next action.

If you don't have the file folders yet, just layer them chronologically in one file or pile or an old shoe box, and keep reshuffling until your hanging files show up.

Be sure to make notes on your cards (about the last conversation you had, future appointments, ranking update) and drop them into your system for future follow-up. You'll be amazed when you open up your files on upcoming days and months, see a prospect, and say, "Oh, yeah, I forgot all about that guy." Without a system, you do forget about that guy, and that's not good for your business: a simple rotating file can make all the difference. Time to move on to B Prospects.

2. **B Prospects:** You buy from these people; you are *their* customer. You have been opening up your wallet and supporting their business—now they get to return the favor. You may or may not know each other's names, but they may recognize your face as a customer. Get in contact with your Bs just like you do with the As; get them all into your system.

3. **Referrers:** Everyone else (think everyone in the world) is considered a Referrer to you. Your warm network can extend out very quickly and grow very big very fast and you can land a lot of business fast—more on this concept in the next section. (Example: Though my sister is not a Prospect, she has referred me to her friends who did buy and became my clients.) This is a hot area to pursue. You do this by *asking* for referrals, and asking your referrals for referrals—this can be very profitable; some say it's the only way (more on this in the next section).

Adding in other Marketing Targets: You can imagine that if you were cold calling, following up on advertising or contacting networking group contacts, how you'd pretty much follow this same procedure. And if you are getting business cards from folks, use those as your contact sheets or cards. Simply write A, B, C, on the business card, make small notes, and get it in the system.

Intentional, Methodical, and Taking No Prisoners

Interesting thing about systems, it's what most successful bigger companies know and use, yet most new businesses, small business, or independent sales people don't use. Hmmm, there's a business-growing clue right there! You need to take it upon yourself to implement systems. If you don't, you'll find it a real challenge to thrive. The challenge is: what systems do you install, what methods do you use, how do you know what to do? These Rewire processes are proven to work. Later you can modify them based on your own unique experiences.

Remember Creative Contact—You'll want to make sure to track information like a person's birthday, likes, dislikes, kids' names, spouse's name, and so on. People

Timmy (son) freshman at U of Minnesota

Loves movies, sailing, travel - ask her where shes been

Libby (daughter) - plays volleyball.

Yankees fan!

find it friendly and endearing when you "remember" things like their favorite sport, or a conversation you had with them, or the fact that they have a daughter who likes penguins.

We've found that it's just a better path—easier and more profitable—to focus on marketing first and then honing sales technique second. I'd bet on a _system_ over individual talent any day—a system creates value in your business and allows you freedom and flexibility. Start a great marketing system first, _then_ ignite extreme profit as you refine and increase your sales ability.

Contacting your prospects and referrers in the right order is crucial. Some contacts are much more valuable, important, or time-sensitive than others. Naturally, those are the ones you'll always want to contact _before_ you get in touch with those who are less important. Every day will begin with you contacting As, then Bs, and (if you have time) finally Cs.

This orchestration of organized creative contact is what makes this system so simply effective.

Leaving the Crowd Behind

Of course, it's great to double your income, but if you're like us, you're always pushing to see what's possible, *what's next*.

What if you want to take it to the next level?

What if you want even more income, more independence, and more freedom? How do you do it? That's what we asked ourselves too. And since we hadn't quite cracked the code that gave us compounding growth and extreme freedom to enjoy other life pursuits while our business continued to produce profit and even grow, we needed to ask a new set of questions. We wanted answers that would produce even longer hang time.

So even though our business was running better than ever, we kept the drawing board up and kept tweaking with the wiring and doing more Einsteins. The answers we found resulted from a series of effective questions that went like this:

"How can we double our business again and have a good time doing it, working no more than we do now?"

We asked ourselves, "Where does our business come from? What's the business that's easiest to land, the best return on investment, and the business we overall enjoyed the most?" The answers were pretty clear and pointed clearly to one common answer: Referrals.

Referrals are by far the easiest business to land, and that makes life so much easier—and they're FREE! So we asked ourselves, "How can we double our business with referrals?" And then, "How do build a system that sends us a steady stream of referrals—forever?"

The answer was, "Build a Massive Referral Network." That answer changed the game.

The Breakthrough

We knew from experience that when you do Einsteins (take four steps back, ask high quality questions) and go at your business with answers and intentional methods that come from your Einstein questions, then add ReMarketing™ and a twist of Creative Contact, you get a big win. We were already doing it. Now we just had to figure out how to do that with Referrals for an even *bigger* win.

The first big ah-ha moment is when we started looking at *everyone* as Referrers. Idea flash! It's as if we'd been walking around blind and now we could see! We'd never really connected the dots completely—we'd never really considered (and pursued) the number of people who are connected to each person we touched? Behavioral scientists tell us that number is somewhere between 150 and 600! Of course, all those 150-600 weren't going to be prospects for us. In fact, probably only a small percentage of these are great prospects, but even a small percentage makes for constant flow of easier sales and a potential goldmine!

The idea was simple; ask everyone we touch for referrals, keep in Creative Contact with everyone and keep ReMarketing™ for referrals turned on—*systematize getting referrals*. No conversation would be complete until we asked for a referral. When we get a referral, we follow it up immediately, get the business and always ask them (whether we landed the business or not) for referrals, and so on and so on. We found that "Ask and ye shall receive" really does work! We started pulling in a lot of referrals, landed business quicker, gained access to contacts we never would have touched before, and started assembling a network worthy of any business mini-mogul. This was the best business we'd ever done! It was eye-opening! We started asking ourselves, "How far can we take this? How big can this be?"

With results this good we shifted from just *thinking* about everyone as a Referrer to actively *targeting and marketing* to everyone as a Referrer—our warm market, cold calls, prospects, clients, everyone. Even if someone said no to doing business with us, we'd still ask them for referrals. (Go to RewireLab.org for the exact words we've found to be the most effective, as well as sales process methods that work.) Of course all these new contacts (Referrers, referrals, prospects, and clients) go into your rotating file system for constant re-circulating follow up. Ranking, ReMarketing™, and Creative Contact systems are still switched on 100 percent and remain critical elements for your successful business-growing method.

How It Works

Now when you look at those traditional methods of marketing and all the people you contact, you think about them a bit differently. You see that each of your contacts now has a lot more value *connected* than previously met the eye. What if you looked at everyone as an active link in your Massive Referral Network?

1. **Warm Marketing:** With visions of building your own Massive Referral Network, you probably now see the opportunity here that 98.5 percent of the world misses. Warm marketing has always been a decent marketing direction, but now it's a legitimate area of serious focus.

   a. **Immediate business**—If you're like most folks who are launching or growing a business, you're probably going to think of about a dozen decent prospects you can contact right away. Chances are you'll land a couple of those right away and a few more down the road. That's where 99 percent of everyone stops—but not you, not anymore. Those immediate seeds of business are just the beginning. You know that you need to catapult beyond the wall of Tier 1. Now, when you ask all dozen prospects for referrals, you'll get referrals and therefore more immediate business. And when you keep asking the more immediate business you keep getting—it's very self-perpetuating and so much easier than not doing it this way. Some of your connections' connections' connections can lead to fantastically lucrative business. Some of the largest accounts we've ever landed have come this way.

b. **Target Referrers**—Because you're human, you also have 150-600 connections. Only a minority may be really great Prospects, but remember, the rest of those connections can refer business to you. They have 150-600 connections too—some are hot prospects, some are excellent Referrers and some are both. (Example: My parents are not Prospects, but they are Referrers, and I've made many thousands of dollars from their referrals and more from their referrals' referrals. Do the math: if you have 150 contacts and they all have 150 contacts, that's 22,500 potential contacts, some Prospects and more Referrers. The next tier out holds 3,375,000 contacts—your network can get massive fast! *When you pursue it.*

> In fact, Warm Marketing has become the best way to build business and make money fast. You connect to high numbers of high value targets in your network that take no advertising to reach and whom you may have never accessed without your warm connections.

2. **Cold calling:** How to get referrals from a cold call—now there's a challenge! Who's going to give a complete stranger solid referrals? Nobody! But because referrals are so extremely valuable, you need to be prepared to play your cards a bit differently when cold calling for immediate business and to come out with referrals. The bottom-line answer is a bit complicated and depends on the scenario, but when you do it right, you'll get a lot of referrals. But whom to target when cold calls are so challenging today?

Because cold calling is much better for marketing than sales, we changed our expectations of cold calls and changed who we targeted. We decided to use quick cold calls for some targets and cold calls to start longer sales cycles for others. The objective is to get as much business up front as soon as possible, while also getting referrals.

a. **Appointments:** To set appointments we use brief cold calls and prefer to establish trust and build more value with an in-person visit or on a later more in-depth call, especially for newer sales people. When you get to the appointment, you must connect, build great rapport and relationship, provide massive value, and ask for referrals whether you get the business immediately or not.

b. **Higher Value Targets:** If the entire sale is going to happen over the phone and it's a bigger target, it's probably going to take more time than one call, so use your first calls to start a relationship, give surprisingly strong value early, and set another time to continue. Also, on a cold call it's easier to get referrals on the second call. Most people (your competition and the Crowd) never make that second call. It's almost like prospects test to see if you call or come back. If you do, they trust you: if you don't, they made the right choice up front.

High value targets are typically more savvy and have more layers to get through before you actually get to speak with them, than the average bear. You need to make sure you understand their motivations (what they want and why) and be prepared to use the right balance of questioning, providing massive value, and leading.

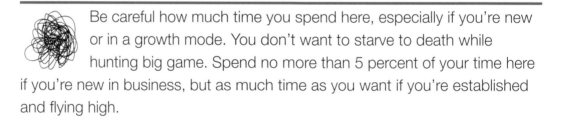 Be careful how much time you spend here, especially if you're new or in a growth mode. You don't want to starve to death while hunting big game. Spend no more than 5 percent of your time here if you're new in business, but as much time as you want if you're established and flying high.

3. **Advertising** (especially print): There's huge value in following up advertising with a phone call as in our previous example with Bankers Magazine—buy advertising and then call attention to it with a phone call. You can also get great response going about it in reverse too, as in the call-first scenario: Place a cold call with the intent of getting information (advertising) into the hands of the recipient, and then follow up with a more meaningful call later. This works pretty slick. All you're doing is probing for simple interest, making sure

your target is qualified (do they buy what you sell, are they interested in what you have to offer, are they willing to agree to another conversation later) and then zipping out materials. The critical piece is to make sure your prospect is a qualified target; otherwise it's all a waste of your time, energy, hope, and materials. You can follow up in person, or, as we prefer, the effective over-the-phone method.

Whether you call first and send materials or call and point out a print ad, the combination and time invested typically builds credibility and trust and helps us have a higher chance of landing the business.

What we don't like:

You may have noticed a variation we don't like—mailing printed material and following it up with a phone call. That's because the odds of the recipient even ever seeing your mail is too low. We spent too many calls describing the mailer to recipients who didn't know what we were talking about. Calls started out on a confused and negative trajectory, and that was bad. We might just as well have never invested the money in the mailer. Go with better methods as we describe to avoid the confusion.

In all scenarios, asking for referrals make sense. If you're targeting pretty well, the person you're talking to is probably a buyer—so the whole conversation makes sense. Therefore, the buyer has some confidence in you and is more willing to give referrals. You've proven that your company has some sort of substance since you have the wherewithal to send a nice piece or to cover the cost of expensive magazine ads—especially when you present yourself as a confident, competent individual with excellent question-asking ability. That leads the prospect to believe you have her best interest in mind. It all comes together, and giving you referrals just makes sense.

4. **Networking groups.** Most people who join groups like the Chamber of Commerce barely scratch the surface of connecting with their fellow members, let alone connecting with members' 150 to 600 connections or the 22,500 to 3,375,000 connections in the next two tiers. Now that you're thinking Massive Referral Network (MRN), it will be easier for you to remember to make those connections.

   Keep in mind, membership in almost any group is an excellent way to build your MRN. You and the referrer have a common bond, being in the same group. There's often a natural tendency to help others with like interests. Asking, "Who do you know?" is almost what you're *supposed* to be doing in these groups. There are some groups (for example, Rotary) where you are told on joining that it's frowned upon to directly ask others in the group for their business. But even with these groups, it's okay, once you establish trust, to ask the group or members for help with connections. All these groups are good ideas. You should be able to connect quickly with all members as well as their connections to find a lot of profitable business when you work it MRN style!

Congratulations, Your System is Collapsing

You know you're doing it right when your system starts breaking under the weight of so many contacts.

When you find yourself wondering how on earth you can add more contacts, keep up with your top 20 percent, and continue to touch base with the 80 percent, you know you're on the right track and it's time to shift gears.

But what do you do?

You wire in automation!

Keep Up with the Latest

 Today, even though we have a system that makes dreams come true, we don't rest. The world changes, so every day we continue to tweak methods and test new ideas in order to stay in the world of prosperity. We suggest you do the same. To keep up with the new methods we're finding, visit our business-building and life design laboratory—www.rewirelab.org.

Method + Automation = Freedom

If you want more business than one person can produce alone, you need to multiply some part of your process. After all, how does one person produce more than one person can produce? Using tools and machines. And if you really want high production and low overhead, you automate.

It's always been this way, whether it's inventing the wheel, going from manual to machine, or from transitioning from sails to steam—you need power, and next you need automation. Thankfully, today there's ready-made machinery for you, and you don't need to recreate the wheel. All you need to do is wire it in properly.

The first rule of any technology used in a business is that automation applied to an efficient operation will magnify the efficiency. The second is that automation applied to an inefficient operation will magnify the inefficiency.

—Bill Gates, Microsoft Founder and one of the wealthiest people ever

Based on what we've seen, Bill Gates is right. If you're doing business basically right, then by all means, bolt an engine on, connect the wiring, and let 'er rip! The results we've experienced are life-changing.

Automation answers the question, "How do I keep in contact with my top 10 to 20 percent while maintaining a connection with the ever-growing number of contacts?" Keep putting contacts in, and automation will handle them all. How big do you want to be? That's how big you can get with method-based automation.

Method-based automation is like compound interest for folks who have been Rewired. Effective automation may also signal your rise to the top of the rewired world—affluent and free.

And like compound interest, most people will say, "Yeah, I get it," but very few practice it. Those who do…wow! The first year I really understood how to operate and manage my Massive Referral Network with automation, I increased my income 250 percent. And since I love to travel, one of the first things I did was start taking my family on cool vacations—something I was concerned about doing earlier in my career because of all the lost sales, lost money, and lost momentum. In reality, one week away costs the average business builder about 2.5 weeks in income.

> "Compound interest is the eighth wonder of the world. He who understands it, earns it. He who doesn't, *pays it.*"
>
> —Albert Einstein

Yes! MRN + automation can increase your business dramatically while you're working it, but it also comes with a monstrous life-enhancing benefit—being able to step away as it continues to work. Sure, it may slow a bit—depending how long you're away, you may earn only 100% of what you used to earn before automation, but you keep the momentum. Your business continues to roll forward even without you.

In my life and business, automation allowed me to set a schedule I designed, and it gave me the freedom I yearned for. The money wasn't bad either—I earned enough to pay off my home in five and a half years! What a happier way to live.

Marketing is like designing a paper airplane. The better the design, the longer it glides.

 Proper method-based automation has long hang time and huge return on investment. You can begin method-based automation on a shoestring budget and evolve into a marketing juggernaut. This is how our business caught fire, grew, and continues to expand today.

Easy Transition, Big Benefits

When you already have an old-school MRN running, it's easy to shift into a high-speed, automated version. You're already familiar with the flow, ranking, calendars, notes, Creative Contact, and ReMarketing™ I've described—all of which continues in the hyper-speed software version. Using software, you can add more fields that will help you take on even more contacts, you can sort the best targets to the top of your contact lists, and you can make easy work of marketing creatively to thousands of contacts. You no longer have to pull your contacts out of hanging file order to ReMarket™. Instead, you simply tell the software to send them marketing messages. It's so easy to find contacts when they call you (or you want to call them) out of order. The right methods plus the right software, and you can create the life you've always wanted.

You know why I love this method?
I've been around the world on it!

—Chuck Fowler, former sales rep, now Rewired FFUSA.com Sales VP

Use Software that Fits the Method

You can spend days, weeks, months—forever—looking for the right software. The choices are mind-numbing. You can go crazy or broke in the process. Basically the type of software you're looking for is called CRM (Customer Relationship Management) software. Since you've been using a method that works (Massive Referral Network), it makes sense to *find a software that fits the method*. (The opposite would mean scrapping a method that can make you a fortune for software with no direction.) Keep that in mind as you shop.

There are some really great companies in this space. Basically, there are two camps; we call them "corporate" and "basement." Corporate CRMs are like Sugar and Sales Force. These are great if you have a traditional corporate structure and a team of technical support on your team who can figure out how to make your software work, keep it working, run around to the rest of your team to try to explain how it works, and then try to figure out why it's not doing what you want it to. Big business loves these systems today, not because the software is easy to operate, but because they know their sales and marketing needs automation to win.

Then there are the tech guys in their basement who see that there's a real need for a simpler CRM. They do build simpler CRMs, but since they are tech people, not sales or marketing people, their software doesn't quite flow right—and it certainly doesn't follow a successful, solid, business-growing method.

In both cases you'll find that software is built by very technical people with good intentions. However, since they probably don't have to live off the results their software provides—like you and I do—they don't seem to understand what features are good and what features are time-sucking black holes. They all seem to "feature bloat"—develop way too many features that just get in the way of making money.

Business-growing, sales, and marketing are high-paying jobs. Struggling to learn software isn't. You need software that works fast and is easy to use, right out of the box. The trick we all have is finding it.

After spending years wrestling with bloated software and with consultants who didn't seem to understand that the clock was ticking, we ultimately had our own CRM built.

 If you'd like to see what we use, you can scan this QR code, or go to www.rewirelab.org.

Shift into the Machine

You've heard the saying, "Garbage in, garbage out!" It's very true here. When you're making this shift, organization is key! It's critical. This is where some very talented and creative people need to slow down and be careful, or have someone else do the data entry.

Simply follow the software instructions and type your contacts in. (Again, perhaps you want someone else to do this for you since it does take time.) Typically you can also import contacts if you have them in electronic format using Word, Excel, email (such as Outlook or Google Contacts), Facebook, etc. By the way, your CRM becomes a perfect central place to store all your contacts for business *and* personal reasons. As easily as you can send a message blast out to all your select business contacts, you could instead send one out to everyone on your holiday card list, or just family, sorority sisters, club members, kids' school connections, friends from a cruise…. This software makes selecting and sending so very simple.

Once you have everyone in your CRM, they are there forever (unless you delete them). Now when you say, "Who was that guy from a few years ago that I met at the conference who was interested in Fiji?" the software will (make certain it does) have a general Search function that will find all contacts associated with the word "Fiji." And BAM! There he is. Found!

When you start out entering people and businesses into Your CRM system, you'll learn the basics. You'll see how entering them into this CRM system will make perfect sense. Get the basics nailed down—data entry, ranking, circulating your files, ReMarketing™—and your system will begin working for you immediately.

Organize Each Contact

For each person in your list of Contacts, put in basic contact information: First Name, Last Name, Phone, Mobile Phone, Fax, Email, Address, City, State, Zip Code. (We call this "Demographics.") Then complete the record by filling in a few more fields that describe what type of contact you're looking at (Prospects, Referrers, Clients, etc.). And then…Have we contacted them before? What are some quick tidbits about this person that are good to remember? Note these for each contact. Also, we'll want to know the quality of the contact and whether we might want to market to them in the future.

 Use your brain selectively, for high income producing activities, as much as possible. Let this machine do the heavy lifting, sorting, and keeping track.

Because you're going to keep in regular contact, you'll want to be sure to turn "ReMarketing™" either on or off. This tells you whether the contact has opted in to your drip marketing. In today's world we are using email along with some (very little) texting for our drip marketing. In the past we've used mail and faxing. You will also shift from your old-school journal calendar to the CRM Calendar, where you can schedule contacts for a call or appointment at a specific date and time and even have a reminder pop up for you. You will also have History, where a record of what's happened with this contact is stored. Last, you'll have a Notes section: this is where quick reference information will be stored. (The information here is the kind you don't want to have to dig through History to find—the little pieces you want to be *right there* next time you open the contact record.)

Six Smart Fields™

From two decades of using CRM software, millions of contact records, and all sorts of data and testing methods to speed results, we've whittled our best system down to six key fields that we are religious about using with every contact. Some fields you've been using already if you've been building a Massive Referral Network with your old-school system, but a few are new, and all are very handy. The below fields are preloaded and ready to use in CONNECT (our software). You'll need to figure out how to load and use them if you're using someone else's software.

CAUTION: As you get more experienced and develop other ideas based on your experience and your business type, you may be tempted to add all kinds of other fields, but do yourself a huge favor and keep it simple. The more fields you add, the more complex your CRM gets, and the more confusing it becomes. Beware of adding your own feature bloat.

1. **Relationship**

   As you can imagine, you're going to be adding all kinds types of contacts in your CRM. Be sure that you label the type of Relationship you have with each (Friends and Family, Acquaintance, Business, Referral, Cold, etc.). You use this field for building a specific list or targeting specific contacts later. For example, I might want to send a personal note to all my Friends and Family contacts ("Hey good news, we just moved to an island in the Caribbean, here's our new address!"). Or maybe I want all my Referrals at the top of my list. Or maybe I purchased a cold list, and I want to call them all. By using this field alone or in combination with other fields, I can get very pinpointed contact targets to the top so I can see and manage them.

2. Contact Type

Further, be sure that you label the prospect *type* (that is, "Client," "Prospect," or "Referrer"). I also use "Vendor," "Individual," "Competition," and "Former Client" for a bit more specific labeling. This way, you know what to generally speak with them about when you call or when you sort contacts into groups to drip market each month.

Later, as you get more experienced, you may want to get more specific as to the type of Prospect or Referrer.

3. Ranking

You know this one. Every time you add a contact to your CRM or open a record (like when you call them and have their record up on your screen), you have the opportunity to add or edit their importance in your world. (This is when you evaluate whether the contact should be an A, B, or C.) I think of it as an evaluation of the likelihood that they're going to do business with me or send me business. The As are likely, so I want to make sure I keep in better contact with them than Bs or Cs.

At some point you may literally have a hundred or more contacts scheduled to be contacted at the same time. What do you do? This is where your A-B-C rating system comes into play. Contact the As. Then move on to the Bs if you get done with the As. Get in touch with the Cs only if there's nothing better to do. (Example: If I want all my A Referrers at the top of my list to call and schmooze, I do a couple of clicks, and there they are.)

So why should you even keep the Cs? Ahhh, this is one of the tricks to building a Massive Referral Network! Most people make one of two mistakes: they either (a) throw everyone who doesn't do business with them immediately into the trash, or (b) try to keep in touch with everyone—and this limits the size of the network they can build. By ranking focusing on As, yet maintaining a connection with everyone else, you can build huge!

When you keep in contact with the Bs and Cs, you allow them the opportunity to reach out to you to do business with you or to send a referral your way. Even if you never call back the Cs, you're going to email them every month. You could end up with thousands of Cs. Keep in contact with them so they *can* do business with you or refer business to you down the road. It's amazing who will call you with business out of the blue when you keep them in the loop.

Does this make sense? Be sure to label them so you can sort them later.

4. **Status**

This code is handy for sorting out where you are in the sales or relationship-building process with each contact. There are those who are in the process of becoming Clients (In Process), or whom you've contacted so far, or whom you have yet to contact. If I'm calling all Prospects, I'll often sort first by Prospects that are As, then further by those I have yet to contact (Not Yet Contacted) at the top of my list, and then whom I never want to call (Do Not Contact).

When I add new contacts, I like to label them "Not Yet Contacted." As I'm doing a call campaign out to them, I make other decisions; I may change the field to Left Message once (LM1), twice (LM2), and three times (LM3), Not Interested Now, or In Process.

5. **ReMarketing™**

You're familiar with this one too! This is a simple (Yes/No) field that indicates whether they have opted in to receive recurring messages (emails, faxes, texts… whatever) from me. Be sure to understand any laws relating to mass email advertising. You don't want to be a spammer nor thought of as a spammer. At best you look shady and non-credible, and at worst you're operating illegally. Do the right thing; it's actually better for your business.

Using combinations of your Smart Fields, you can separate all your Prospects into groups and ReMarket™ to them with the right message. For example: your Active Clients will get a message that includes a thank-you for doing business, a promise of your commitment to continue to provide the best, and of course a suggestion to refer business to you. (We are, after all, constructing a Referrer Network.) A Potential Client, on the other hand, needs to get a different type of message—maybe a few testimonials accompanied by an offer to do business with you—and of course a suggestion to refer business to you.

6. **Date of Last Contact**

   This is a field that I like my CRM to enter automatically after each time I contact a target, but if yours doesn't, then figure out how to enter it yourself. Here's why. If I have thousands of Referrers, Clients, and Prospects whom I contact every month or so, I want my CRM to put them in order so I can make calls to my top targets immediately—with only a couple of clicks: The one I just spoke with recently should be at the bottom, and the one I spoke with the longest ago should be at the top. I don't have to use much energy thinking about who to call. I just click and call—my energy is invested in creative communication, not thinking about sorting. This field is a huge. When you use it, you know exactly who to call 1st, 2nd, 3rd… 69th…and so on.

If you buy software that doesn't include these smart, proven, money-making fields—*that work the way we just discussed*—you'll need to figure out how to add them, add drop-down choices, and make them work. All CRM software companies have extensive manuals with directions, tutorials, and tech people to help you figure all this stuff out. Or you can use ours—you already know how. Yes, it's a shameless pitch, but ours works, and that's good for you.

Other Fields You'll Love

Birthday: Everyone loves to get a call on their birthday. Even if you don't get them in person and have to leave a message, call them.

Title: It's nice to be able to sort by CEO or Marketing Assistant or whatever.

Keywords/interests: Entrepreneur, football, travel, Porsche, animals, Fiji…. If you enter keywords you'll be able to pull together groups of like interests in the future.

Other Functions You'll Love

Calendar: As you are speaking with any of your contacts, you'll identify some who need to be contacted again at a specific date and time. Your CRM will have this functionality. Every morning you'll open your contact manager and get to work. The very first thing you'll do is take a quick look in your calendar at who's queued up for you to talk with or visit at a certain time. And of course the only way these contacts show up at a certain time and date is because you set them up that way. When you have more than one person to contact at the same time, you always contact the top-rated first (A).

Notes: Again, a field you know from old-school marketing. Notes are little reminders that need to be at hand when you make a call so you can impress with the personal facts that you "remember" about them. When you call up and ask how Timmy is doing this fall at the University of Minnesota, you will be scoring huge on the rapport and relationship scale!

As we showed you earlier, great notes might look like this—>

It's these little things people (your targets) enjoy. "Remember" them without having to remember them: use Notes!

History: Every time you open a record and have a conversation, you're going to make an entry about that conversation. Make your entries brief and effective (abbreviations you won't remember end up meaningless, and writing a novel is a waste of time). We've found that "effective" means a sentence or two unless there's a legal or medical reason to make a long entry. These entries simply add more color and information to give a more complete profile of the person

Timmy (son) freshman at U of Minnesota

Loves movies, sailing, travel - ask her where shes been

Libby (daughter) - plays volleyball.

Yankees fan!

you're targeting. Remember, knowledge isn't power, but the use and application of knowledge is! The more *usable* your information is, the more profitable it is for you. Try to keep only information that will make you (or save you) money.

Connections: This function shows you who's connected together. Husband and wife, relatives, business associates. It's a great way to "remember" how everyone fits together. It's like actually applying social networks for business-building purposes.

Groups: Groups are people who have a common denominator. You can assign people to a Group like relatives, friends, frat brothers, bankers, bankers with a specific bank, club members, tennis lovers, Green Bay Packers fans, people I met in London, Christmas Card list, little Timmy's play group, investment bankers—most any reason you like. Then you can click open and contact—easy, easy, easy.

Everyday Use Of Your CRM

With demographics and your six Smart Fields, you can serve yourself top targets. No more mystery about who to call when: your system has it all ready for you.

Slice, Dice, and Serve: Filter and Sort Functions

In addition to the ideas already listed above, here's why CRM software is better than a hanging file. You can pluck specific contacts or groups with common denominators out of circulation immediately, no rummaging. Pull them out fast and get to them fast. It's amazing how many people you can contact so quickly and effectively.

Example 1: If I have 30 Prospects whom I have yet to make contact with, out of a total list of 1,467 contacts in my CRM, then I need to be able to quickly filter out those 30 into one short and easy-to-work list.

I'd filter like this: Contact "Type = Prospect" AND "Status = Not Yet Contacted." BAM! There's my list in about three clicks—easy. As I'm calling the people on this list and making contact, I'm updating my Smart Fields. I'll be paying attention to "Rank" and labeling as I go: A, B, and C, so I can find my top prospects fast later. As

I'm making headway and it looks like we're doing business, I'd change status to "In Process." And when we do business, they become a "Client." If I decide they are no longer a "Prospect" because they don't buy what I sell, I can switch their Type from "Prospect" to "Referrer," because you always want to ask for referrals, even from those who are not clients, right?

As soon as I make any of these changes, this target's place in my network has changed, they're either hotter or colder (A, B, C, In Process, Do Not Contact, Client…) or different (Referrer rather than a Prospect). Now they'll show up higher or lower in my Prospect list, or they'll show up in a different list, like Referrer or Client. Everyone is being weighed, nurtured, and sorted—I can find and work them all easily. Using the Smart Fields method, it's all very effective.

Example 2: Let's say I want to keep in contact with the best people who send me business. I wanted to contact all Referrers ranked A, and I want those whom I have not contacted for the longest time at the top of the list, and those I've contacted just recently at the bottom. Simply filter by "Type = Referrer" AND "Rank = A," then SORT by Last Contacted Date.

Example 3: Maybe I want to contact all clients in Kentucky, except the ones I really don't ever want to speak with again. Easy! My sort would be "Type = Client" AND "State = Kentucky" AND "Status does NOT = Do Not Contact." The result is exactly what I wanted; a very organized, very surgical, and very effective list. Now I can use it to contact them very quickly.

Example 4: Let's say I wanted to invite all my contacts (except undesirable people) in the 612, 763, 952, and 651 area codes to hear and meet a motivational speaker at my office. We'd filter: "Area Code = 612" OR "763" OR "952" OR "651" AND "Status does NOT = Do Not Contact." BAM! There's the list and I can contact everyone, fast!

> **Example 5:** Let's say I wanted to send an email to all Referrers. Wow, that's a big list, but easy, and I bet you could figure it out. Remember to exclude all the "Contact code = Do Not Contact" or those with "ReMarketing™ = No." Don't send emails to people who don't want them!

With the above lists I could make phone calls, merge letters, print envelopes or labels, and send emails...whatever I want. It's all there, and it's easy to produce. It gets kind of interesting and fun. Without a CRM, how would you do any of this? How could you accomplish as much as you need to in such a short time? You probably couldn't, and you'd miss your dream simply because you didn't know how to effectively use the technology that is at your fingertips.

Quick Pre-Sorts

There may be lists you work regularly or targets that you contact frequently. Most CRMs have sorts that you can save. With one click, you can create a list to work from. It's like presets on a radio. Man oh man, it's slick! Talk about saving your brain for the tasks that matter.

 Go to www. rewirelab. org, or use the QR Code to see how we use sorts.

Monthly Contacts and Drip ReMarketing™

Now every month you can intentionally, methodically, and quickly generate a list to call your top 10 to 20 percent Contacts. You'll start with Contacts that give you the best chances of generating money (As that are Prospects), then contact others in accordance with your plans (Bs that are Prospects, As that are Referrers, or Cs that are Prospects—your choice). You do this by being able to sort your list. Your CRM will be able to do this very nicely for you. It's a basic function that you'll use...a lot.

You're probably *not* going to call everyone in your list every month for three reasons: (1) You only want to invest talk time with top targets; (2) you don't *want* to contact some—they're not worth your time, or they told you every two months is good; and (3) as your list grows, there's just not enough time to reach them all (especially Cs).

 If you don't run out, or get close to running out, of As and Bs to call, then you don't have enough good contacts in your network. Time to import high quality lists or get a bit more aggressive asking for referrals.

But not to worry about not reaching everyone by phone. Just email everyone who has opted in. (Be sure to understand what "opting in" means, and the requirements involved. There are laws regarding this, and you *must* adhere to them). With Referrers who have sent Prospects to you, consider sending them a thank-you of sorts, or treat them more like "fans." Those who have yet to send you business may end up getting a message that includes the benefits to them or the benefit to those whom they refer. Both sets may get an update about what's going on in your industry or a case study that demonstrates your unique ability or value without looking like an advertisement. (Make sure this information is interesting to the recipient; otherwise, they will find your monthly contact boring and end up deleting everything you send or not even looking at it.)

Make your communication *brief* (two sentences is my preference) and *interesting*—you just want them to lean in with curiosity. Switch up what you send. What I mean is, you should send just a text one month, then send a cartoon the next, and then a short article after that. Switching up your messages makes each one of them more interesting to the recipient. Now, rather than sending a boring newsletter that is specific to nobody, each group gets a slightly customized message. You're actually demonstrating to them that you value their time and understand their specific interest by being short and specific. Even if they know exactly what you're doing, they'll still appreciate your effort.

 Everyone loves newsletters, right? Nope. Some people absolutely despise them. They feel they are written to be broad, so they cover everyone—and therefore no one. Send brief, targeted, and specific information to each recipient. Demonstrate that you understand their individual interests and that you honor their time—they'll appreciate you for it! More on this and very specific marketing techniques in my next book.

Import/Export

Import simply allows you to bring in lists to your CRM rather than having to type each record individually. It's a handy way to bring your contacts over from places like Outlook, Google, other CRMs, Excel, and even places like Facebook. And it's a great way to buy a list of targets and then work through them to find As, Bs, and Cs.

Export allows you to move a copy of your data or lists out of your CRM. For example, your CRM may not be able to email or print to your custom contact lists, so you'll need to use some other software for marketing or mailing. You'd simply filter and sort, then export the list, and finally *import* the list into the other software. Also, if you ever want to copy your contacts out to be able to change systems easily, you need to have an export function.

Don't get freaked out by "import-export" talk. As with everything, there's a learning curve, but it's short. Yes, you're going to screw it up a time or two, but you'll get the hang of it. Just remember, most people (the Crowd) won't do this because there is some challenge to it. They'll either never try, or they'll give up. But if you accept the challenge and grasp the system, guess who will be left standing to reap all the rewards? Yep. It's you. So figure it out and be around to see yourself win!

Advanced Contact Information: Swim with the Sharks

In his book *Swim with the Sharks Without Being Eaten Alive*, Harvey Mackay, one of the world's greatest businessmen and most-admired CEOs (and endorser of this book), lays out what has become known as the "Mackay 66." These are 66 pieces or fields of information that he likes to know about a business target or client. He uses this information to both land business and stay in Creative Contact with his clients. Mackay has built a business, a reputation, and a fortune using this method—literally a fortune.

You can do the same, and you can start with 6 Smart Fields ™. Later, like Harvey, you may be interested in adding more data, such as political affiliation, sports interests, wife's name, kids' sports, and so on. You'll add more contacts and start connecting them into Groups that you can tear through: you'll link Referrals and Referrers and add Drip ReMarketing™ tracks. If you're so inclined, you can delve into all that much deeper in my next book—it's all about taking **Massive Referral Marketing** to the hilt.

Your Daily JAM!

Most people use the word "work" for the activities they feel they *have* to do all day to make money. Usually they don't like what they do, and they don't like their work. The word "work" ends up with a negative connotation. So let's not call the action of creating a cool life for ourselves "work."

In fact, if your life consists of more than about two or three hours a day of activity you don't like but feel you have to do, maybe you should consider a little Rewire—directing your passion and energy in a more happiness-congruent, life-designed direction.

If your job is creating and building the life you love, you'd probably do it all day and all night, and you'd do it for free—*that's* not work! Sure, there are challenges and drudgery in life, but when your job is creating, building, and compounding your income, business, and life, it's bigger than any "work" could be. Test looking at your job through a new lens: "I *get* to do this today!"

"Born to fish; forced to work."

—Bumper sticker

JAM! It's What the Rewired Do

As I'm sure you've already noticed, there's a special term we use when we're talking about the focused energy and effort we direct into every day driving business, growing a Massive Referrer Network, and creating our dream.

That term is...

JAM!

What it means is this:

The time we do nothing but JAM! It's the time we devote exclusively to building, expanding, and operating. We are in the zone; we're focused; it's game time.

When I'm jammin' I am devoting myself entirely to my objective. I don't want to be disturbed by anything. When you're jammin', you're building. You're growing. You're achieving. You're on your way to making more money than you've ever had before and creating the kind of lifestyle that you've been dreaming of. Jammin' takes focused concentration and dedication—and it pays off in a big way.

Jammin'! Challenging? Yes, sometimes. Worth it? More than I ever imagined. This is where you really get traction.

Keep your JAM! time sacred, and nothing can stop you!

Wire in Daily Rituals!

Time and time again, we hear it, "Use your time wisely. Time is your greatest asset. Blah, blah, blah…." But sometimes using your time most effectively is a trick because *you don't understand exactly what "using your time wisely" looks like.*

If you've never actually *seen* super effective use of time, then how do you copy it? How do you know what to do? Most of us operate the way we've seen others operate. That's fine, except that most people we see don't operate on a schedule *designed to achieve, let alone be, Rewired!* They operate like the Crowd. If you want to achieve, or be part of the Rewired elite, you need to be regimented. Regimented doesn't mean militant or bad or uncomfortable. Regimented means intentionally doing the basic things every day that you need to do—that's it! Like JAM! time. JAM! time is a ritual. I mean, really—since you're alive and you're going to be doing something anyway, why not make what you're doing for a few hours a day super effective? The end results will usually more than double your income—and that means funding a much better quality of life.

What if you really played full-out, really lived it? What if you actually *got* your dream rather than just dreamed? How would that feel?

Success, achievement, and becoming Rewired take doing things that most others don't—like JAM! Building a Massive Referrer Network and going stratospheric with a Rewired CRM—that can be a bit scary if you've never done it before. But it's absolutely critical to achieving the life you're really here to live. I mean, really, so many people think that they are just supposed to be naturally good at things (marketing and sales and business, for example), and if they aren't finding success right away, well, they figure they must not be cut out for this stuff.

And Marketing? We're "taught" that you warm market, cold call, place ads, network, or whatever. Of course we've gone through those exercises and realized that we're only given part of the puzzle. Those who don't get the reveal, like you have here, end up grasping at straws. The Rewired find these methods that work and then they turn their work into a cookie-cutting machine on high speed.

The big successes are achieved by those who prepare, act, and learn, and then continually repeat that process.

If I've made that sound like a daily ritual—well, that's exactly what it needs to be. And the ironic part of it all? Rituals actually make building easier! The fact is that most entrepreneurs, intropreneurs, marketers, and salespeople don't really do the basics well because they don't have a structured method to follow. Take referrals as an example: Most of us don't even ask for referrals on a consistent basis—or ever. Instead, we make a sale and say thank you and that's the end of the story. We don't connect the dots and make selling, building, and growing a methodical achieving process. The Crowd puts in hours upon hours of struggling and chipping away at things very ineffectively. They simply haven't focused on using their time effectively. So, the masses miserably grind away rather than prospering. Why? Sometimes, getting ahead may mean doing something different from what they already know, and that's uncomfortable for some, but after two to three weeks it feels normal. Amazing: most people won't Rewire for just two to three weeks to get on the track that they've always wanted. **Will you?**

Do your rituals everyday—even if it's not what the Crowd does. Remember, wealthy people do what normal people won't. Make yourself proud. Get in control.

Massive and Focused Energy to Launch, Little Energy to Maintain

To start out, realize that no matter how you decide to end, you need to get up to speed as quickly as possible. You need to create momentum. Like an aircraft, you need to put forth considerable (massive, colossal, gigantic, immense, huge) energy to get off the ground and begin flying. Then when you're up to speed and at the right altitude, you can throttle back and keep flying easily. That's how it works.

Launch into your day visualizing that you're going to sprint every morning from 8:00 or 8:30 AM until about 1:00 or 1:30 PM, then pace the rest of the day with sales, wrap-up, and networking. The degree to which you are driven to get to the next level in your life will determine how aggressively you attack. It's very possible to achieve more in 7 to 10 years at an intentional Rewired pace, with methods and systems that work, than most people achieve in a lifetime. We see it happen for all kinds of people. We're living it ourselves, and so can you!

> "We don't have an eternity to realize our dreams, only the time we are here."
>
> —Susan Taylor

71

Zero To Hero: The Schedule That Does It

This is the standard business-growing-mode schedule that we use at our businesses, and it works. Here's basically how we arrange our days Monday through Friday. (Saturdays, maybe we make a few calls, but not many; and on Sundays I recommend not taking or making any business calls at all.)

This schedule is based on B2B sales. When my prospects were People (P) and not Businesses (B), then my JAM! time was Tuesday through Sunday, 3:30-8:30 PM. If you're doing B2B sales, just revise the schedule so that you're always contacting your targets when they are most likely available—the principles will be the same.

First Things First

As you're Jammin', you're operating under the money-making procedure called "First things first." The most important actions are taken care of first. Only after those timely and important actions are completed do you move on to actions that are less important. If your job is to build a fortune and you could do things that earn $1,000, $200, or $50, which would you do *all the time*? The $1,000 activities, right? That's why you're going to label every contact A, B, or C. That way, your CRM knows what the important things are, and it can sort them for you—First As, second Bs second, last Cs. First things first. It's the way of the Rewired.

Here's a typical routine if you want to be one of the Rewireds who get 80 percent of all the good stuff, including the money!

Rise, Shine, and Get Ready

Pre 8:30 AM—Do some light exercise or stretch, and eat breakfast. Even though you prepared for today at the end of yesterday, open up your CRM and look at your calendar. Get your mind around today.

8:30 AM - 1:30 PM—This is in-the-zone time. Period. This is game time, baby! Nothing, I repeat, absolutely *nothing* besides Jammin' should be going on during game time. This truly is like a sport. You planned, you trained, you're here to win. Now do it!

Do you practice during the game, or do you play the game hard and play to win? If your aim is to win, you play full out. If you do anything else—anything, like surf the web, install software, drive, watch TV, call your friends, or anything except first things first—well, you're just not going to produce enough to achieve the lifestyle you want, and you can never be free.

Here's what to do and in the order of importance:

1. Scheduled calls—outbound/inbound*

2. Outbound calls to A-Ranked Prospects

3. Outbound calls schmoozing with your A-Ranked Referrers, then B Prospects or Referrers—your choice.

* Inbound calls (unscheduled). Always take calls if they're going to make you money! These will happen at any time of the day. For sure, chunk similar activities, but when the phone rings or someone walks in the door and it's a potential sale, I'd push my grandmother down the steps to get that call and make that sale. (I'm kidding about Grandma, but very serious about getting that call.)

Snacks and Breaks

Regardless of what I write below, you must adhere to any doctor's advice above what I recommend as a schedule and diet. Do what's right for your body.

Eat breakfast before you begin, and throughout the JAM! time, sip water and eat snacks to keep your energy up. If you work well with things like caffeine (I admit to enjoying espresso), then have it handy so you don't have to take time away from Jammin' to get it. We all benefit from short mental breaks (we like 5+/- minutes of break every hour) in this five-hour sprint. Reward yourself for Jammin' with a nice little break, stretch, oxygen, and a snack.

1:30 PM—Lunch and exercise. Yep it's later in the day than for most people, I get that, but we are taking a late lunch *by design*. You'll find it's easy to do if you've been fueling with snacks and water (oh, and maybe an espresso or two), and you've been taking mental breaks. You'll be feeling pretty strong and great through all of this. What I've found is that any time taken away from your sprinting Jammin' time is going to have a compounding negative effect. And I do mean negative, as in not in a good way: it's going to reduce the quality of your life. I'll JAM! it out, thank you very much. Hope you do, too.

Being regimented—it's huge! It's a lifestyle design choice, and it makes a meaningful difference. Remember what we discussed about the surge of energy an airplane needs to lift off? What would happen if your pilot reduced power to only 60 percent upon takeoff? I can tell you that I have no interest in being on that plane to find out. I'm just not going to take the risk. Same thing with my business. What about you? Keep the acceleration on until you're at 30,000 feet and well on your way!

For most of us, a half-hour lunch is enough. Remember, it's still game time. Do you see pro athletes eating a huge meal at halftime? No! They'd be puking their guts out all over the field or court shortly after they got back to the game. Same here. If you take too much time, you will get sluggish and your brain will talk you into doing things that are not good for you, for your

"The difference between what we *do* and what we are capable of doing would suffice to solve most of the world's problems."

—Mahatma Gandhi

brain, or for your future. You really have so little game time to create your cool lifestyle, especially if you're looking to have it sooner instead of later.

Remember, you can easily achieve more (including having more freedom, fun, and more cool) in seven to ten years than most everyone achieves in forty. That's what happens when you're a regimented Jammer.

2:30 - 5:00/5:30 PM—This is where I love to go to scheduled sales calls and meetings, or get paperwork done and agreements buttoned up. Finally, at the end of the day, I like to arrange things (schedule, desk, car, calendar...) so that I can hit the ground running in the AM. Yes, it's 5:30, and I did suggest strongly to break that mindset, and we are doing that. We used every little piece of our day very purposefully and targeted our best time when targets are most receptive. The rest of the world runs on 9:00 to 5:00, and they've gone home, so now it's time for us to shift gears too.

At the end of my day, I know I gave it my all. Most people give it just enough to get by and wonder why all they end up with is…well, just that—enough to get by. Do what you want, but my job is to show you what works on the aggressive plan that gets you a cool life that you say you want.

After 5:00 PM

Everyone has their preferences and the way their body works. I like to hammer out a hardcore workout (if I didn't already do it at 1:30) between the time I'm done with Jammin' and family time. Frankly I need to burn off some of the extra energy I've churned up throughout the day, and exercise is a great way to use that energy to better my health before I interact with my family. What my family needs is more loving energy, not the kind that comes from a Rewired Jammer being all amped up from the day. Also, with a workout I get a very fit body in the process. Sweet!

You can modify your schedule before and after JAM! time to meet your current needs. For example, my exercise schedule has changed over the years depending on the ages of my kids. When my kids were younger, I'd get up really early (like 5:30 AM) and get in my workouts so I could coach (or attend) the kids' sports events at the end of the day. Also, as I'm writing, I'll do a workout after JAM! time (between

1:30 and 3:30). The end result is using a time when my natural mental energy is low to do physical exercise. After exercising, my brain is oxygenated, and the creative process writing requires is easier.

Evenings and Weekends

This guide is about lifestyle design, not being a workaholic. You need to design evenings to fit what's important for you at different times in your life. Evenings for me depend on what my kids are doing. Is there a game? Am I driving? Am I coaching? These activities are my first priority. Hey, in a few years they'll be off doing things completely unrelated to me, and I won't see them for big chunks of time. Since I love them with all my heart, I want us to be together while we can.

Given the above, there are sometimes real opportunities for business in the evening and on the weekends. And if you approach this like a business (not like work),

Whatever you do, do it with purpose

then you want to build fast. Jammin' by day and *some* networking by night can be good business-building strategy. There may be very beneficial events to attend in the evenings or weekends. (As I write this section it's Sunday, and I just finished participating in a four-day event in San Jose, California, that was wildly valuable).

The end of the day is *not* JAM! time. You're not going to be directly making money at this time of day, but you still need to use this time effectively. It is a great time of day to do important things to get you ready for JAM! time, like plan, read, write, study, or install software.

Saturday Morning

Saturdays are like evenings, different strokes for different folks at different times of your life. I have three boys, so over the years Saturday has taken on different shapes.

Saturday is often a sports day: I often coached, and I always attended. Depending on the kids' schedules, I've had to adjust mine to make sure I accomplish all the things I need to do. So let's say my son has a tournament and there are three games. Often, I'm the guy out in the car between the games on my laptop or making a few quick calls—not in a stressed way…in an effective way. Hey, this is life. Get it all done and have fun with it! Just a few years into this schedule, I had options and flexibility most of the world never sees. So can you.

Back before I understood automating a Massive Referrer Network or CRM, Saturday morning used to be the day I'd send mailers. I'd literally drive to the local post office, wait in line Saturday morning, and hand my stack of mail to the person behind the counter. (I mailed about 200 to 300 pieces per week.) Then and only then did I know that my mail was in the right hands. I do not assume that just because I put mail in a box somewhere it's going to get picked up on time, or at all. My success was way too important to leave anything to chance.

and balanced effectiveness.

No, standing in line at the post office for 45 minutes on a Saturday morning does not seem like a good use of time. However, if you consider that I needed mail to hit recipients Monday for greatest response, and the only way to assure this was to hand my mail over the counter on Saturday, it was *very* effective to stand in line.

Today we don't send mail like I used to. I might do a few other things on Saturday morning, like messing around with my CRM Software or putting contacts in it for more effectiveness during JAM! time. Maybe I'll sort and ready lists for email marketing, write, and plan. For me this isn't work; it's interesting and exciting. I know that what I'm working on will get response, and I'm building. I may do research about new markets, read a little about bettering my technique, take a seminar…or, like now, write. Whatever it is, I'm doing something that fits in with what I feel excited and passionate about.

A Day of Rest

If you want affluence, success, freedom…and health, then take time off. Our brains need a break. And what good is having money and success if you're not happy and healthy? Personally, I need one full day off, and for me Sunday is perfect. It's after Saturday, which isn't a Jammin' day, but it is a thinking day, and it's right before a Jammin' day. Sunday is a great day to let my brain rest. When I *do* work seven days with no break—even on things I love—it seems that one of the days the following week turns non-productive. And I think, "I should have relaxed on Sunday." Interesting, isn't it? Give your brain, body, and life a break—take a day of rest.

Go on Vacation and Take Big Chunks of Free Time

Because you use your time so effectively, it's as if you bank time. Later, when you want or need to use time for any reason, it's there for you to spend. You have plenty of time for things you didn't expect to happen. Now you can go without the fear of, "Oh, I shouldn't go—I have too much to do." Go. You've paved the way for your life to be more flexible when you need it or want it. Now you can both prosper and take guilt-free vacations for big chunks of time. Go. Enjoy. You deserve it! Bank time—it's a great way to live.

Energy Cycles—How The Rewired Use Them to Advantage

For best results, you need to JAM! when the timing is right for *your Prospects* too (when their energy is up and they're at a place you can reach them).

You want to reach your Prospects before they get too involved in their world and their day and have too many mental files open. If you wait too long into the day, your prospect just has so little mental energy left, you don't get the focus you deserve—and they're more likely so say, "I have to think about it." What they should have said is, "I'm too tired to make this decision right now. You should have caught me at a better time when I had more energy."

Would you rather contact someone who can't take it anymore, or get them when they are alert and positive and receptive? I'd want the latter: it's effective, the most profitable, and it's what will fund my lifestyle and my dreams. It's the way dream-lifestyle Rewireds do it. And now that you know what works, JAM!

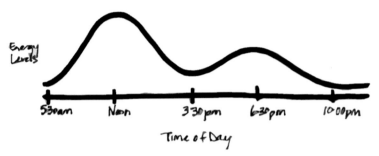

Understand human body energy cycles and use them to your advantage. You have probably experienced how your body energy is up and down at different times of the day. Throughout the day you've got energy, and then you don't, then you have it again, and then you lose it again. Most people are in the more energized part of their cycle and rhythm in the morning, and as the day progresses that energy dwindles. Those cycles exist for you, me, and our prospects. So, you need to be doing business when you are energized and your prospects are ready for you.

If you're doing B2B sales then your Jammin' time is your high-energy time (8:30 AM to 1:30 PM, and before lunch). If you're doing business with consumers (people at their homes) then your Jammin' time sweet spot is more like 3:30 PM to 8:30 PM. You've got to do business when your target is alive and alert…and when they're somewhere where you can find them.

Fuel Timing

We've found it best to intentionally have lunch later than everybody else. We've found that having lunch after JAM! time comes with big benefits. Here's the big reason why. At about 1:00-1:30 everybody else (the Crowd) is just coming back from lunch and feeling very tired and sluggish, and they aren't even done with their version of Jammin' yet. They opted to use prime time for eating. Can you imagine using prime time for eating? It's bizarre. Now they're faced with an uphill battle mustering enough energy (when their body is using energy for digestion) to finish out their sprint. Good luck. It's too damn difficult. Rewireds have no interest in it.

While the Crowd begins their uphill struggle, we're smiling and feeling good about ourselves because we jammed effectively—now we can go have a nice lunch or exercise feeling great about our progress.

Look at lunch as a transition marker. When you're done with lunch, move on to a different set of intentionally blocked actions. You may not even come back from lunch—you may be out and about buttoning up business. You may just end up really liking this life.

And on the topic of lunch, eat food that's good for you. Think of eating as a pit stop in the Indy 500. Pull off the track. Relax. Fuel up. I use the term "fuel" on purpose—if you want a great life, then use food as fuel. Know what different foods do and don't do for you. It's important—you must understand it. If you're going to expect maximum performance from the system, are you going to pour jet fuel into it, or are you going to use a crappy low-grade fuel? Here again, I have no interest in riding in an airplane someone just filled to the rim with soda and donuts—we'll never make it to where we want to go.

After you eat, go for a walk or do some sort of movement or activity for just a few minutes to get your system warmed back up and ready to roll at high performance. When you walk or do squats (no weights, just regular ol' squats, 20-40 of them), you'll be ready to kick it—you'll be clear and ready to roll. There's a Chinese proverb that says, "A man who takes ninety-nine steps after eating will live forever." So don't go disrespecting an age-old proverb; use it. It works.

Is This Conversation Going to Make Me Money?

Have you ever had time where you need to be Jammin' and someone just insists on taking you off course? These distracters are not on the same lifestyle track as you. You know the people I'm talking about! They call you in the middle of the day and talk about nothing. They'll stand at your desk, cube, or office entry and suck the life out of you and drain your resources. They *don't understand* that you're on a mission, you're directing your time and energy with intention and focus, as if it's the most valuable resource on Earth. Your distracters will drone on, talking about the weather, the news, the internet, gossip, their aunt's most recent sickness, food, kids, girlfriends, Mexico, you name it. Beware of it, and nip it in the bud—or give up your dream. You must release the distracters' grip on you immediately.

We've found two effective ways to deal with these situations.

One way is to go easy on the other person. The other approach is brash. The "nice" approach goes like this: say, in an urgent voice, "Oh, hey, I really gotta make (or take) this call." Then rush off. Or grab the phone and start making a call, or say, "Hey, I gotta take this call." And then make or take the call and continue your JAM!

The brash approach? It goes like this: look the other person straight in the eye and say, "Is this conversation going to make me money?" Hey, sometimes brash works. If you say it in the right tone, with a smile or even without a smile, the recipient gets the message. He or she will probably never waste your time again.

When I began sharing this line with people on my team, and they thought I was getting a bit long-winded, they'd ask me, "Hey, is this conversation making me money?" Don't you just hate it when someone uses your own material back at you! Okay, okay…I got their point right away. It still happens from time to time, and I smile, turn away, and quit wasting their time. We all do it in good fun, and it has turned into our subtle little cue to get back on track and moving forward.

Save Yourself!

Today I see people whose jobs and futures rest squarely on performance (for example, business owners, sales people, entrepreneurs, anyone whose pay is affected by performance). When they're hanging out in someone's doorway, talking about things that are obviously sidetracking both parties and costing them a huge amount of money and possibly their dream, it seems like a real shame. Someone needs to shout, "Is this conversation going to make me money?!" Let that person be you. Be the one who saves yourself…and others.

> Be the one who saves yourself…and others.

Set your rules and make sure everyone around knows they need to leave you the hell alone so you can do what you need to do. And you need to leave them alone so they can achieve their dream too. I know, I know, it seems innocent enough to chat, but there are plenty of structured times throughout the day for that—do it then. Or do it before or after Jammin'! Honor your time and others' time. Allow yourself and others the greatest opportunity to live the dream. Time is critical.

Jam when you've got the energy—it's what the Rewired do! Use this natural energy to your advantage by making as many calls as possible in this zone. That's when you're highly effective (i.e., profitable). Outside the zone you're not as productive (i.e., unprofitable).

Keep on asking yourself: "Is this conversation going to make me money?" If the answer is no, get back to what does.

This is the "It" in Nike's "Just Do It"

When building their business, most of the Crowd seem to make about 30–65% the number of contacts per day that they need to. Then they wonder why things aren't working out for them.

Strip this schedule down and really understand what you're accomplishing during your JAM! time. Here's the trick: For me and so many people who are in business-building (launching, growing, expanding) mode, I found that it takes about 20 to 35 (your industry may operate differently) "meaningful conversations" per day—by the way, that's 7 contacts per hour. Keep track with little tic marks on a piece of paper. Dependent on the quality and effectiveness of your conversations, that may mean 100 to 200 calls a day. The better you get, the fewer calls you need to make.

8³⁰-9³⁰ ||||| ||
9³⁰-10³⁰ ||||| ||||
10³⁰-11³⁰ ||||
11³⁰-12³⁰ ||||| |
12³⁰-1³⁰ |||||

Part of being regimented is making yourself do this. Your competition won't, and they'll eventually lose, drop off, and quit. Meanwhile, you'll be thriving!

Often, winning isn't a function of being better; it's just being more regimented and simply outlasting everyone else. Successful people do things normal people won't.

Sometimes it's not that the winners are better than others; often it's just that they're more persistent. How's that for a secret?

Now that you know the number, keep to that pace. It may sound like a lot, but that is what gets your business really cooking. If your promise to yourself and your family is to be earning the money to live your dream, go after it with great enthusiasm and intent! Break through to the life you want—it's all there, all you need to do is do it. Make those calls. Get out of your head about it and just get the job done—that's what Jammin' means.

You must track yourself, keep data, analyze results, and tweak for better performance. As you are in launch mode, building mode, or growth mode, plan on contacting 20 to 35 Prospects or Referrers every day in your five hours of JAM! time. That averages out to be about twenty calls an hour, so one call equals about three minutes on average. And you can expect that you're only going to get a hold of four (at first because you're learning) to seven (when you're experienced) people out of that twenty, because everybody has different schedules and some people are out of the office and all that kind of stuff. This works for most whomever you're contacting, whether it's the people on your prospect list, referrals, appointments, family members, or anyone else. Remember to call them at the time of day that gives you the best chance of reaching them.

Let's assume, then, that you're talking to twenty contacts each day, because at the very minimum, if you're following this, you're going to have 20 to 35 solid people a day to be able to talk to about your product or service. And not just gate-keepers; you'll be talking to decision-makers who are Prospects or Referrers. (In my next book, which is all about taking **Massive Referral Networking** to the hilt, we'll be targeting Joint Ventures too—a lot of them.) Some of these contacts you've made will yield you sales immediately—literally, right then and there. You need to be aware of this and always be working toward that end result. But many contacts will yield appointments, and some will need to incubate. As you're making these calls, be sure to use Smart Fields ™ and work your contacts accordingly. If you have a method that works, a system to operate that method, and a strategy to build your lifestyle, it's so much easier to make it all happen.

If you've done this the Rewired Elite way, you will be adding 100 to 150 good Prospects to your sales funnel and Massive Referrer Network every week. And at 400 to 600 per month, after 6 months you've got 2,400 to 3,600 new prospects in the mix. I can tell you for certain that 99.9 percent of the population, which includes your competition, does not do it this way and is not achieving these results. This is a highly regimented schedule that works. Use it.

Sh#!t Happens. Plan for It!

(My editor really doesn't like it when I curse in print. He feels it takes away from the message, and I agree…except here.)

To assure you stick to your plan and have the life you dream—get insurance for it.

Stick to a regimented daily plan that ensures success even when the unexpected (sh#!t) happens. In fact, count on sh#!t happening. So plan and stick to the plan. For example: if you stick to your plan Monday through Thursday, but something happens on Friday that won't allow you to do what you had scheduled for Friday, that's okay. Completing your daily regimen properly four out of the five days of the week—for at least two of the four weeks of the month—will probably be enough to keep you on track. However, when you decide to get up late Monday, and Oprah's on Tuesday and you've just got to see it, and then something happens Friday…well, what remains is just not enough time, energy, and effort to get your amazing lifestyle off the ground. That hit-and-miss schedule will get you a pay-by-the-day and a bring-your-own-sheets hotel room at the poor farm—simple as that.

Avoiding the Sh#!t

So…

Number one: You must continually guide your thinking to the positive. I know it's a battle for all of us—this isn't the way the world has conditioned us to think—but you need to be aware when your thoughts drift to the negative and pull yourself back on track. Work on this as if your life depends on it, because your life does depend on it. In real life, this means extra activity that most people won't do. But then most people (only the happy and fulfilled) really are not intentional about their life. You'll need to make sure you're clear on what drives you (why you're doing what you're doing). Maybe it's just that you want to have a cool life and be able to do all the things you want to experience. Maybe it's a red Ferrari. And…

Number two: Do unfathomable, Rewired things (the Crowd will never do this) like plan your schedule the night before, get up early, and make sure all your systems are loaded up and warmed up and running so that when the gun sounds, you're ready to roll.

Number three: Just do what's queued up to do. Run the entire race. JAM! It's very simple, but very few do it. It's critical…and it works.

Andy Doesn't Work Fridays

People ask me if I work Fridays. I wouldn't call what I do *work*—especially on Fridays. I love to use that *Friday feeling* to be especially light-hearted and creative. Fridays are great days for being productive—the rest of the world is in weekend mode and doing very little. I prefer to use that sliding-in-to-the-weekend feeling to fuel my passion to do what I love to do—build and expand. I find I get more done on some Fridays than other days simply because I've got fewer people wanting my time—they're already into the weekend.

Back when I was first getting started I would JAM! (you'll notice I don't call it work) all day

"It's the little *details* that are vital. Little things make big things *happen*."

—John Wooden, Hall of Fame NCAA basketball coach with 10 titles in 12 years *and* into the evening every Friday. For the first few years I was relentless! And over time, like when I was learning how to connect a Massive Referral Network or CRM, I'd go very aggressively and then celebrate when I was done or when the project was flying.

Even today when I have a new project and I'm driven to get it up to speed, I run a very deep and intentional pace for long periods of time (no more than six days straight, otherwise the next week suffers). But I reward myself along the way, and when I'm done, boy does the accomplishment feel great! Last spring after a big project I jetted to Paris for a concert and spent five days of fun exploring the City of Lights.

But what do *you* want? Let's compare two stories. Back in 1989, I started in the Merchant Services industry. The same week I started, a guy who would become a very dear friend of mine (we'll call him Andy) started too. We were trained exactly the same way and had exactly the same opportunities. On Fridays, Andy would say things like, "I bet nobody's going to be around today," or "I don't think it makes sense to go out cold calling today; I bet people are taking off early." Eventually, he was right because the end of the day came, and he'd made no new contacts and zero sales.

I remember looking at him on Fridays, shrugging my shoulders, and…I'd go Jammin'! And after I was done Jammin', I'd pick up my weekly mailing list and head for home to put address labels and stamps on my mailers that I'd hand deliver to the post office on Saturday. Some Fridays lacked for sales and contacts, and I thought of Andy enjoying an early weekend, but others were banner days. I took every inch of opportunity I had to move forward. Because of that, Andy and I went down two different paths.

Today, Andy is still working the same way and still getting what that gets you— nothing special. He'd love to have more money and he'd love more freedom, but instead he struggles. After all, it's what people do, right—struggle? They're not there on Fridays, they don't leverage Saturdays, and they certainly don't come on Monday prepared for the week, excited, and ready to JAM! But Andy is doing what the Crowd considers right—or normal. True—most of the population is grudgingly punching the clock yearning for the end, for retirement. But that's not those of us who are serious about *really* living our dream. You will take advantage of every precious second to get one step closer to your dream. Funny thing is that it really only takes a couple of years doing what normal people won't do to be on the track that fulfills your dreams.

For most, it's ever-elusive—just a dream. But for those of us who think, plan, and *do*—that "dream" evolves into our day-to-day real life. It's true what they say, today is the first day of the rest of your life. The thing is, how do you want the rest of your life to look? Go that way! And never look back! Run!

Why Most People Don't Get What They Want

Do you want to know the number-one reason why most people don't win? It's because they quit.

Every day we see it: people quit, and it's game over, dream dead. Business isn't like the Olympics where only the top three get awarded. You can come in last in the top 20 percent and still have more money and freedom than 80 percent of the population. Much of success is a mental game—you're battling with your self-talk. Most of us are in our own way. It's not someone else that prevents us; it's us.

We've already learned that your plan isn't going to go as planned; it's going to go the way it needs to go so you have a cool life. So if it takes twice or ten times as long to reach the goal of living your dream, isn't that better than never living it at all? (And it *could* take only half as long!) There's a saying that I never really understood until I understood persistence, and it goes like this:

"Life is a journey, not a destination. Enjoy the journey."

As it turns out, life really is too damn short, and we spend way too much time stressing and toiling over all the stuff we *think* isn't going right—when, actually, things are going perfectly according to the plan we just don't understand. Trust!

Trust that you are on the right track. And you are—as long as you're massively acting and working on yourself and always striving for the best.

Hang in there and keep doing your best, and you'll beat, by outlasting, damn near everyone. Persistence beats who you know, where you went to college, who you marry, how good-looking you are, how smart you are. Persistence beats everything. Period. Done. End of story. Ya wanna win? *Never give up*. Wanna win fast? JAM!, regiment, and test other methods with 10–20% of your business. Keep pushing, testing, tweaking, and never quit. You will break through.

Trapped in the Crowd, or a Record-Breaking Life— Which Do You Choose?

"To have the level of success that I want to have, it's difficult to spread it out and do different things. It's such a desperate, obsessive focus—you just really have got to focus with all of your fire and all of your heart and all of your creativity."

—Will Smith, actor

The reality is this: you can design your lifestyle to be anything you want it to be. But that's also where the trouble begins, because knowing the world is your oyster means that it can be distracting to get specific and decide exactly what you want. How's that for an odd downside of being able to have it all? But it's true. You must focus if you are going to get what you want. Not only have we observed this regularly in others, but I personally know this to be true. I was the poster child for being distracted by the next shiny thing. Doing more than one thing at a time, I lost years of progress in my learning experience. Once I focused, I started making serious money—almost immediately.

Focus First—Diversify Later

It's common to think, "I found three things that can make me $50,000 each. So, I'll just do them all and make $150,000 a year." Right?

Wrong. Do them all, and you'll be lucky to make enough to buy lunch. That's what happens from lack of focus. There's just not enough time in a day to do so many things, and you'll never be able to give any one thing the attention it deserves.

But you may think, "I found these three things that interest me, and if I choose one, I'll lose the other two." True. But if you choose to do all three, none will prosper. There's a good chance that all three are good options if they fit your goal. So, make *one* a wild success. Success comes from focus: do only the things that matter, and forget everything else. After you're wildly successful, then you can diversify—that's how money is made. Diversification comes *after* your first success, not before.

What if I Miss Out?

Creative people are notorious for being afraid to commit. What if we choose the wrong road and miss out on something better? Choose, focus, and give it your all—one thing at a time. Later, after you've made money and had success, you can come back and do another deal—or hire a high performance team to do it for you. No need to be greedy and take all the opportunities. They'll still be here if you choose to switch and focus on those other ones later.

Allow yourself the opportunity to make a commitment. Realize that *after* you choose, you'll need to focus and push through various curves in your learning—that's how success happens. Big success may take three times longer than you originally expect. But you'll never have successful results, not in fifty years, if you're working on more than one thing at a time.

John Lennon Didn't Sell Insurance

The Beatles were focused musicians, and look what it got them! John Lennon was a driven musician and songwriter, he lived for the music. John was focused—driven in one direction. You didn't see him opening an insurance agency on the side just because there was money in it! I'm glad he didn't: imagine the world without the Beatles. So be a Beatle! Get focused, be obsessed with your dream, and live a cool and focused life!

I had a guy the other day offer me consulting services, and what he was saying really made sense, and I was getting excited about contracting with him. However, at the very end of our sales conversation we drifted into other topics, as conversation sometimes does, and he pulled out two other business cards for companies he represents—that's three different companies he's trying to focus on! His consulting services immediately lost value to me because I understood that *he* didn't understand the value of focus. I later decided to thank him for his time, but bow out of contracting his services. Lack of focus hurts you because it doesn't work. Experienced people will see your lack of focus and lose faith in you.

Big Money Flows to Experience

The people who make money in most industries are the ones who have taken the time to earn experience. They've invested the time, paid attention, and gained the know-how. They have more ability in their little finger today than they did in their entire being when they were inexperienced. Now they have an active network full of connections and the experience that helps them recognize the good deals and separate them from the bad ones. They know the right and wrong things to do, what isn't being said, and how to read between the lines. Experienced people can read that experience in one another—they know when they're dealing with experience or inexperience.

Not to say there's no opportunity for new people in a business—there's tremendous opportunity! The top of the heap is never crowded, and you can get there fast! Just understand that making real, sustaining money in any business takes *experience*. The phenomenal news is that you can virtually compress time with fast-paced and focused doing…as you're learning in this guide. You can accelerate to the top fast by jammin', being regimented, and just doing.

There's a saying:

Success comes from good judgment;
good judgment comes from experience;
and experience comes from bad judgment.

The only way to make it through to success is by *doing*.

We see this every day in real life.

Here again, from life experience, I've found that's exactly true. I've landed some really large and insanely profitable deals, but none of them came right off the bat when I was new in a venture. Often they did "fall into my lap" as referrals, and therefore they were also relatively easy to land, but that happened only after I had gained experience and people knew about me. (They knew about me because I promoted the heck out of myself through my Massive Referral Network and CRM—and did a great job, so the Referrer was confident in my performance!) Big deals and big money rarely go to novices in any field, and those big deals are often referrals.

Quit!

Ever hear that saying, "Winners never quit, and quitters never win"? Quite true—if you quit too early, too often. Use this saying more as guideline than a rule though. I'm *for* quitting in many circumstances. Nearly all opportunities can be given a very fair trial in as little as ninety days. Other opportunities may require six months, or maybe a year, but rarely more. After six months of serious action, you usually know what you've gotten into—and sometimes you know earlier. But if you've given a business a full, fair trial and it's not for you, then you have to seriously question yourself and evaluate why you're hanging in there.

For example, a buddy of mine, Todd, turned me on to a business opportunity selling medical supplies, like face masks, latex gloves, and hair coverings—basic stuff you'd see a doctor or surgeon wear. He introduced me to the wholesalers, and he showed me who in my market would buy these products. He explained his pricing and invoicing, and he even gave me an outline of the sales process. All of it was really fairly easy. So I went into business.

With Todd's direction I purchased enough inventory to start, then launched into the business with massive action. The business took off quickly, and I had clients who would order regularly. Basically it was a decent little business built on a consumable product. (I love consumables because clients always have to keep ordering more!) I had regular customers, business was growing, and I had ideas for some custom packaging. The downside was inventory—this inventory took up a lot of space. The money was okay, but not that great, and the margins on all that inventory were skinny. I'd have to move *massive amounts* of product *forever* to buy the lifestyle I had in mind. The other part that didn't excite me was that, though I had the advantage of handling a consumable product, it was heavy, and I was the one who had to deliver that product. Keeping up with deliveries meant I took time away from getting more clients (sales). Alternatively, I could pay someone to do the deliveries, but for a fledgling business, that eroded too much of my profit. In sum, this business required moving product around—getting it, stocking it, selling it, and delivering it. Moving product meant time on the road, which I've found to be low-paying. (No offense, but some of the lowest-paying jobs are to people who transport or deliver product.) I knew that the money was in selling, and that moving product took me away from selling.

Bottom line: This business also wasn't conducive to the flexibility and freedom that are part of my dream lifestyle. And, frankly, I wasn't passionate about selling rubber gloves. So I decided it just wasn't for me. I'd given the business a very fair shake, and I felt I knew where it was headed—I just wasn't passionate about it. I sold my inventory back to the wholesalers and my client base to a competitor.

Don't quit too soon. But, understand, it's okay to quit if you don't like it, it doesn't suit you, there's no future in it, or it's just not going to take you where you want to go.

The Clock is Running

It's natural to ask, "How long does success take?" But if there were an easy answer to that, then everybody would be marking their calendars and coasting until then. I really don't know how long it will take you specifically. *That* mystery is where most people get a bit freaked out, bail out, and get a "good job" that gives them "security."

For a better answer, let's get better perspective and context. We are not talking some pie-in-the-sky, fictitious, unrealistic, get-rich-quick scheme. We're talking about reality. I have no interest in showing you a technique that doesn't work. You need to have your mind right with your vision *and* reality. Know that you can have everything in life you want. Also understand that it will not come overnight. But no matter how long it takes, it's a hell of a lot better living your dream than not, even if it takes a while to get off the ground. Agreed?

Now, the chance of hitting a home run exactly as you imagine right off the bat is about zero. And that's okay—it's how everyone begins. I suspect that before reading this book you had a different business plan and perhaps now it may have shifted. Next, you need experience

"But I want an Oompa Loompa now!"

—Veruca Salt,
Charlie and the Chocolate Factory

94

operating the system. Only with experience will you hit a home run. The only way to get experience is to do, and to do, and of course you need to start.

The next typical question is, "How long do I need to *do* before I'm experienced?" In *Outliers*, Malcolm Gladwell says doing anything 10,000 hours will mean you're among the best in the world. 10,000 hours—that's 200 weeks at 50 hours per week, which is about 4 years working full time to be the best in the world! 4 years! That goes to show you how people with drive (like you and me) can rise fast. Gladwell cites all kinds of examples, including the Beatles and Bill Gates. The Beatles, for example, played more gigs together before they had any widespread attention than most bands ever play together in their entire careers.

The point is that it takes time…and specifically time doing and jammin' on your craft. So, let's say you're on a learning curve that takes four years, but the investment of those four years allows you to break free. Would you trade those four years on the learning curve and the freedom it brings for a lifetime of wishing you would have? If you're saying to yourself, "I'll invest the time to get what I want," then you're on the right track. You've been Rewired.

And there's even better news. You don't have to be the best in the world to make $100k+ per year, and you don't have to be the best in the world to make $1 million per year either! What you do need to do is provide so much value that people appreciate paying you well for doing what you

"People usually way *over*estimate what they can do in a year, and way *under*estimate what they can accomplish in a decade."

—Tony Robbins

enjoy. Whether you want to be the best in the world or simply fund a pretty cool life, the recipe begins the same way. It's, "Hey, I'm hopping off here; this is good enough for me." That hopping-off point is unique for everyone and yours to choose.

When you stick in there and figure it out, you own it. It's yours—no matter what. Ask yourself: "How long should I give it before give up on my dream? Or if I was really serious about living my dream, how hard would I play? What would full-out playing look like if I were serious about achieving my dream?"

I always ask myself, "If not *now*, John, when?"

With this guide, you now have a method that's proven to speed results. All you need to do is add *you*.

Getting the Combination Right

Remember as a kid at school, trying to get your combination lock open? You'd try and try, and finally the darn thing would click and pop open! Finding your business growth groove and funding your dream lifestyle is kind of like that. You'll try a combination that seems right, but it probably won't work quite the way you imagined the first time. What's really cool, though, is that unlike a combination lock, with success *there isn't just one combination*—it's not all or nothing, open or closed. Instead, you're actually learning and earning while you're figuring out how to get the lock open. And there are multiple ways to make it work—this guide should cut that learning time way down and pop your lock open much faster.

So, don't give up if you don't succeed wildly right away. It just means you tried one combination and discovered that *particular* combination wasn't exactly the key. But there is this thing that will create success for you if you really do it: it is a three-letter word that begins with J and ends with M, and you have to apply it every day. So *JAM*! Keep trying, don't give up, and you will find the right combination to unlock success.

THE

secret in life is to keep trying different things until it works. Most people give up before they

FIGURE IT OUT.

—Jay Abraham, marketing legend

When the Money Comes

But let's follow this timeline a little farther down the road—assuming you stick it out, funding your lifestyle design while your friends are still *working*. Though your friends have advanced their careers, there's really only so far most will ever get—and honestly, it's usually not that far. Most people advance a couple levels in any industry and then level off. And then they're in a rut—stuck in the same job, spending what they earn and unable to earn much more. They end up settling for mediocrity and a lack of control over their job security. We all know a lot of people in this situation—it's about 80% of everyone. It probably isn't how they envisioned living their lives, but it is what it is, and that's that. They toil away their lives in jobs they really don't like, without a whole lot of fulfilling opportunities. They feel frustrated and start looking forward to retirement.

The Rewired, on the other hand, have been chiseling away, learning, applying knowledge, building, and growing. They have been silently building and compounding momentum, and as they financially roll past their friends, at first nobody notices. But a couple years later, when they do something visible (like buy an awesome house or car, or travel around the world), all of a sudden the working-life friends ask, "Who died?" They think maybe you inherited all kinds of money—but no, it's all you!

Time for you to smile and give yourself a pat on the back! It's *all you.*

Nobody can take away what you've learned and how you can apply it to live your dream. You are now equipped to do whatever you want in life. You can live where you want to live, you can travel *when* you want and for pretty much as long as you want. Your family has all the things the Crowd would love to provide for the people they love (things they can't afford), and when you're ready to retire you can have all the comfort, space, security, and care you choose. When you own this ability, you live life on your terms—you're living your life the way *you* designed it.

Why Doesn't Everyone Do This?

Everyone doesn't do this because they don't have the confidence to step away from the Crowd—thankfully. Otherwise there would be a whole lot more competition for you and me! We all know that in life there are no guarantees. Some people equate designing your lifestyle with living a risky life and having little control—usually because they see the Crowd fail from lack of methods that work. For those of us who wouldn't live any other way, it's more like having complete control. We'd rather have the knowledge gained by doing Einsteins, testing, Jammin', and steering our own way than any other way we can think of. We know how to market, build a network, automate, communicate, build rapport, sell, and follow through. Those are very transferable skills. If we ever wanted or needed to go out and get a job, we have what every employer is looking for.

Job Security

Having real understanding and transferable skills—being Rewired—*that's* job security…for life, my friends. That's control and freedom in any economy. With that knowledge and ability we can write our own ticket, anytime, anywhere, and that feels a lot like a guarantee to me. Contrast that with friends who took a job out of college and were laid off, fired, or transferred. Sure, they had good jobs, but it sure seems like a crappy, out-of-control, no-guarantee life to some of us.

If Not Now, When?

Trust yourself. I mean really. You've done an Einstein and asked yourself what you really want in life—and now you're clear. Maybe this is the time in life where you should pull out all the stops—what do you think? If not now, when? If other people can do it, then so can you!

"Remembering that I'll be dead soon is the most important tool I've ever encountered to help me make the big choices in life. Because almost everything—all external expectations, all pride, all fear of embarrassment or failure—these just fall away in the face of death, leaving only what is truly important. Remembering that you are going to die is the best way I know to avoid the trap of thinking you have something to lose. You are already naked. There is no reason not to follow your heart."

—Steve Jobs, 2005 Stanford commencement address

Life Can be Good...*Really* Good

My sincere desire is that this guide has added massive value to the direction you're taking and the methods you're using to achieve the life you dream. I hope that after reading this, you understand that you can design your own path.

You don't have to, nor want to, follow the Crowd to be "successful." You don't have to get a "good job," and you don't have to work your way up some corporate, government, or family business ladder hoping for the best. You can accelerate around those above you or create your own ladder. You can design your own roadmap and live your own plan. Through a combination of decision, commitment, and running methods that work, you can create the machine that will fund your lifestyle design.

You can have it all and on your own terms. Your life is yours. Design it. Live it. Savor it. Love it.

Just imagine...life the way *you* designed it!

20

years from now you will be more disappointed by the things you didn't do than the ones you did. So throw off the bowlines. Sail away from the safe harbor. Catch the trade winds in your sails. Explore. Dream.

DISCOVER.

—Anonymous

Your Winning Ticket!

You hold in your hand your winning ticket. What I have shared with you are the discoveries that have taken many of us where we wanted to go—and we keep learning, building, and growing. Now it's your turn. This isn't a lottery ticket idea, a one-in-a-million chance of winning. You've already won—all you need to do is live it! Here you are, in this place and time, and for some reason life has placed this guide in your hands.

Now it's your choice. We all have opportunities that come along in life. Will you recognize this one and seize it, or will you close the book and say, "Someday I'll…"? Today is the first day of the rest of your life, my friend. Use it, love it, give it a big hug and squeeze. Jump up and shout, "Yes! Let's do it!" Decide once and for all that you're going to live your life. I mean, why not?

If you continue on a manilla course then you get a manilla life…and a pang of regret at the end of your life for what you didn't do.

Grab your dream. And when you get hold of it, never let it go!

"Take one step in a new direction and you're already living your new life. Stay on that path, and you create real-life magic."

—John Eliason

Dedication

Thank you to everyone who has read these pages as the story was being written—and thank you to everyone who has supported me, taught me…and even tricked me. I wouldn't be where I am without each and every one of you.

A big hug to that little kid that was me many years ago, and an encouraging smile to me the younger man who yearned for a teacher to show him the formula for what really works. And to the man who strove to figure it out and kept reaching for what's next. To be able to go back in time and tell the struggling me, "Keep after it, it all works out, keep doing what you're doing, you're on the right track." I am so thankful that I persevered when it would have been so easy to quit.

But first and foremost, this book is really for you. It's *your* turn now.

What's Next?

Every one of our experiences shifts our understanding. There's always something next.

I Made a Common Rookie Mistake

A few years ago, I was working with Jay Abraham (think, brilliant mind; you may have heard of him), and he said, "You need to write a book."

"But what do I write about?"

Then he said something that's stuck with me like it was branded onto my brain. He said, "I believe that if you've figured something out, and others are searching for the same answer, it's your moral obligation to share it with them."

Yep, that cinched it. I started writing—aggressively.

After I'd written and written and written and rearranged what seemed like dozens of times, I hired an excellent editor (Ed) to help me smooth out any wrinkles and firm up my book. Ed the editor told me two things: "You've got some real gems here," and "You made the rookie mistake—you put too much in one book; what you've got here is about three or four books." Argh.... What that really meant was that we needed to figure out how to make three awesome books out of one monstrous encyclopedia of knowledge.

This also means that I have tons more to share with you— enough for a business-growing trilogy. But really it doesn't stop there either. After all, I go toe-to-toe with the world every day, just like you. From me, you get both what we've *found* and what we're *finding* as we reach for what's next. So what comes of all the information that is in the other two books?

How I release this information out to the world has yet to be determined. Perhaps it is in book form, maybe it's classes, and maybe it's the Lab.

All I can say is, "Stay tuned."

There's More—Much More—to Share With You

Case Studies that you can cut and paste into your own marketing—this makes life and business easier!

Tricks from the road—these are techniques that you only learn from doing—a lot. Talk about speeding up your learning curve!

Urban business growing myths—most of what you hear, learn, and see in business is pure rubbish. It's just not what it appears to be. There are ways that work, and then there's what most people do.

Insider email marketing methods—screen shots and processes all queued up to show you how to do exactly what we describe in *Rewire*.

Social media marketing. Turns out it can be a big deal—but it's not how I thought it worked. And it's not how most people are doing it.

Joint Ventures—sexy, yes. But they don't work, at least not the way most people think they do. Not even close. You can make a fortune, or completely miss the boat. We do JVs all the time, but there's a trick to it.

The game. Your network is your net worth—the game is expanding both. The question is, "How fast do you want to do it?"

I can show you how to extend your network even further as you continually build and add on to your Massive Referrer Network. I call it your Massive Referrer Network on steroids. You can even hire others to make the calls to build your network—I did.

The right tools for the job

Because we're very active in business, we continue to test products, practices, software, and methods. Stay connected with the Lab so you get the inside fast track of what's out there and what our experience with it has been. Rewire Lab is a growing encyclopedia of experience that you can use to speed your dream.

Go to the lab and sign up to get the latest. You'll get every new bit of information we post, delivered directly to your inbox. Get it and test it yourself—I love to hear about the coolest tests and breakthroughs.

 Go the lab to see what's happening right now—type in www.rewirelab. org, or scan the code.

One tool you must get right is your Marketing software....

Success is a high-paying job.
Struggling to learn software—that ultimately doesn't get you the lifestyle you want—isn't.

- John Eliason

You need tools that work fast and are easy to use, right out of the box. You don't want to have to monkey around with tech, and you don't need any more struggle— you want simple, powerful, and profitable. The trick we all have is finding that right system. After spending years wrestling with bloated software and with consultants who didn't seem to understand that the clock was ticking, we ultimately had our own built—a stripped-down, ready-to-race, easy-to-use, powerful suite: marketing, sales, advertising, and analytics. It's all based on *Rewire* and it's all ready to use "right out of the box."

Now, the very same software we use, you can use too.

Go to the lab and check it out. There's probably even some special incentive when you get it through *Rewire*.

Check it out—type in www.rewirelab.org.
Or scan the code at left to connect with us.

Whatever You Decide to Do

Whatever you decide to do with your life and business, what would happen if you went about it like you needed it—like you need air!

Interestingly, all things are attainable, and you can actually become pretty much whatever you want to be. But it's hard to change our habits and easy to let things slide—or quit. After all, you can always get by just fine being part of the Crowd.

But what if right now, you made the decision to be the man or woman you imagine you'd love to be? And what if you really did it? I mean, pure and simple, just did it. How proud would you feel? Kinda makes life pretty awesome, doesn't it?

Our job is to share what we're finding and ignite your curiosity. Your job is to make it happen.

Welcome to the first day of the rest of your life, my friend.

We're in this with you—right now.
Scan the code at left to connect with us.